Don't Cramp My Style

A Campaigning Life

Simon Cramp

Contents

Dedication

Simon and Adrian

My brother (on the right in the photo) was a great bloke who lived life to the full and took on the world at swimming and smashed it in the world of learning disability sport. This is what my dad said about him recently at his funeral:

> Frustrating, stubborn, grumpy, annoying, irritating, exasperating, delightful, funny, caring, considerate and generous, these are just some words that describe Adrian. A truly complicated man.
>
> Adrian was born in Lambeth Hospital in London just after 9am on Sunday 15th August 1971. He was just 8 minutes later than his

twin brother Simon. Even their birth was an event, as they were born, not in a delivery room but in the lecture theatre as the birth was being viewed by a number of trainee midwives and doctors who had to see a multiple birth. They were born a month early, and they stopped breathing for about a minute at their birth, and this was the cause of their difficulties. A few days later their Grandpa Gordon described them as two little peaches! When Adrian came home from hospital he was so tiny, less than 2 bags of sugar, that he had to be fed every 3 hours, a process that often took 2 hours, so there wasn't a lot of sleep taking place.

Adrian had a great childhood, and loved playing football and cricket, not very well, but who cares! School was a nightmare; he didn't always get what he was being taught. Nevertheless he got through it, with a few GCSEs. One of the highlights of his school was when he and Simon were selected to run a stretch of the Queen Baton Relay for the Commonwealth Games. In 1985, family holidays at the seaside usually started with a panic event, losing Adrian. But often he would be found standing, fully clothed and up to his neck in the sea. He couldn't swim!

After school he attended Chesterfield College on a Sports Leader Course, organ sing and taking part in various charity events. This led to him going to a supported employment with a local council, in the Sports Development Department. This was both a joy and trial. Shortly after starting work it was found he couldn't swim and one of the swimming teachers took him in hand, and Adrian learned to swim. This turned out to be his greatest joy. This led to him being selected to swim in the UK Special Olympics at Cardiff in 2001, as part of the East Midlands Team , gaining a number of silver and bronze medals .He was always rather miffed that a mere fingertip stopped him getting a gold medal. He also represented Great Britain in a swimming gala in Geneva, Switzerland, again gaining a silver medal. Adrian decided that he wanted to gain swimming teachers qualification, but he was told that his employer wouldn't support him taking the exam as they didn't think he would be successful. This is where the stubborn part of his character took over. Without saying anything to his employer he took himself off to Skipton in North Yorkshire one weekend, and with a little help by someone reading him the questions, listening to his answers and writing them down, he gained the theory part of the exam. A few weeks later he persuaded me to take him down to Huntingdon where he took the practical exam, again passing. He gained the full certificate and proudly presented it to his manager the following Monday. They paid all his fees shortly afterwards.

Due to reorganisation Adrian moved to work in the community based at Ash Green Centre and then at Ringwood Centre. One day he was setting off to work, and whilst on the bus felt a bit unwell. He got off the bus and felt much worse. He had the wherewithal to call an Ambulance, and was found to have suffered a heart attack. It is true to say that this event was the start of Adrian suffering long term health issues.

Adrian always seemed to be on a time delay, he was usually about 10 minutes behind everyone else. He had little concept of time. If he had an appointment at 9.30 he would appear at his front door a few minutes before, seemingly not grasping that the journey would take time. His cooking usually ended up under or over cooked as someone else would take his attention, he was a typical man could only do one thing at a time!

Adrian needed a lot of help from people and he really did appreciate that help. It may not help always have been obvious as he could moan and groan. He could be quite grumpy but as was commented recently HE WAS OUR GRUMPY ADRIAN.

When I phoned him, it was very rare that he would answer. I found out that he would turn his phone onto silent so he wouldn't be disturbed! Mind you the phone would switch to answer phone and I would be treated to the longest greeting message ever recorded, inviting me to leave a message.

Adrian over the past few months had began to lose some of his memory, and often I would get a call from him about something. We would talk about it and decide what to do. However ten minutes later I would receive another call about the same thing. This could happen a few times, and I know that I could get a bit cross, sorry Adrian.

He was one of the most generous people I know, he was always willing to offer his family and friends anything he had, and most visitors would often leave clutching a bottle of water he had insisted they take. He was also very vulnerable, and could be taken advantage of through his naivety. He was really pleased when he sat with his niece, Abigail, and taught her to count up to 10, although 8 was always missing.

We know that Adrian had many health issues, and unfortunately these had become his main thoughts. Most conversation with him centred on his health, and he had become more and more reluctant to leave his home. He loved to watch the Sports Channels where he could indulge his passions for cricket and Manchester United.

He relied heavily on his twin, Simon and the boys had a very close bond. They strived for individuality, but were linked closely. They felt each other's discomfort, when one was having some form of operation. They would argue and get cross with one another, but of anybody else argued with one of them, the other would support their twin.

Adrian was truly a very complicated person; he needed a high degree of maintenance. He wasn't always logical, and could be difficult to understand. He often didn't quite get that what he wanted couldn't always be met straight away. Yet he had a wonderful smile, a cracking sense of humour, a kindness towards people in distress and loyalty to his family and friends. We will always miss him and I think many others will.

He is at peace now and we picture him sitting in a better place with the one person he always missed, his Mum.

Just one more thing, to paraphrase Spike Milligan, Adrian always told us he was ill and he was.

Forewords

From David Brindle of The Guardian

Thirty years is no time at all in the scheme of things. Yet it seems an altogether different era when you look back to the 1980s and reflect that we were still sending people with learning disabilities to long-stay hospitals as a matter of course. We've come a long way since then. It's easy to forget that when you despair at the state of things: the brutal cuts we have seen in the welfare state to pay for the banking crash a decade ago; the continuing struggle of disabled people to secure their rights as equal citizens; the shocking hate crime that anyone who looks and sounds different is always in danger of suffering. There is, indeed, much to despair about.

But here's a cause of celebration: a book by and about someone born with a learning disability, albeit not especially severe, who was one of the first generation to be not at risk of being consigned to hospital for good and who has gone on to lead a rich, rewarding life and to make an important contribution to the emancipation of disabled people. Simon Cramp is today one of the most well-known figures on the national stage with, as we now say, "lived experience" of learning disability. He is knowledgeable, articulate and able to hold his own in conversation – occasionally heated discussion – with government officials and ministers. Under the terms of the 1944 Education Act, passed in living memory, he might well have been considered "uneducable".

His book is idiosyncratic, emotional (especially when he discusses his late and beloved twin brother, Adrian) and frankly a touch disorganised. Very much like Simon himself. If you're looking for a scholarly tome on learning disability, put it down now. But if you want a fascinating insight into one man's acceptance of his disability, and his mission to make things better not just for himself but for hundreds of thousands of others, read on.

From Jonty Rix, Brian Rix's son

Before I met Simon I had heard about him. My father spoke highly of him and how he had helped him win over the Mencap conference. I have subsequently worked alongside Simon on a couple of occasions and have always enjoyed his company and been impressed by his networking skills and the insights he offers. It is hardly surprising that people have always got very nice things to say about him!

Don't Cramp My Style is a really interesting read. It provides an insight into Simon's life and many of the UK's most important social changes in the lives of people with learning difficulties in the last forty years. It is at times moving, thought provoking and funny. It introduces us to many different people who have played an important role in the field in recent times and it shows us how they have been influenced by Simon. The book serves as a clear reminder why the voice of people with learning difficulties must be heard in so many areas of society, not just in relation to issues that are deemed to be relevant to them.

I know that Dad would have been delighted to read *Don't Cramp My Style* and not in the least bit surprised that Simon had produced such a valuable book.

From Tim Keilty, the Editor

I've known Simon for a few years now, usually bumping into each other at conferences. It must be a year or so ago at the launch of the Learning Disability Alliance at Portcullis House that Simon asked me if I'd help him with this book. I obviously said yes, perhaps I'd had a drink. It has been a great experience, reading about what others say about him and gaining an insight into his life.

Everyone comments on Simon's great networking skills, his ability to digest policy and fire it back at the powerful, and his desire to improve the lives of others. He has been inspired by others but as this book shows, he himself is a great inspiration. I've learned from working with him on this book that he is also a hard task master!

The best bit about this book for me is that, from Simon being someone I bumped into once or twice a year at conferences, we are now great friends.

Chapter 1 **About Me**

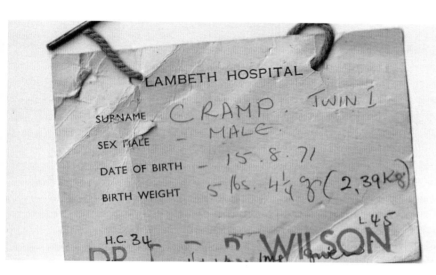

Twin 1

My late twin brother and I were born in August 1971 in South London, where my parents lived. My Mum retrained as a medical secretary and my dad was a police officer, more about them later in the book.

I also have a younger brother and a sister and brother in law, my sister has two children to whom I am an uncle and my young brother has a daughter. I have aunts and uncles who live in Peterborough and Bristol.

When I was born I stopped breathing, and was rushed to the Special Care Baby Unit, in the hospital in Lambeth, South London, where I was resuscitated, initially this did not seem to present as a major problem, and as I grew the difficulties began to present. My brother and I would be dressed in the same clothes as each other until we were about 11 years old, the same socks, the same green jumper and shorts. My brother and I talked in a language that made sense to us but no one else! As I grew to the age of 11, my difficulties began to become more apparent.

I entered education prior to the 1981 Education Act, and therefore did not have the benefit of Educational Statementing, and as such I had to manage in mainstream education. I did receive very good support from the majority of my teachers, and my late mother and my father would spend hours each evening with homework. I was bullied at school by my so called peers, usually due to my inability to do the simple things, like catching a ball; a task I was unable to do until my early teens, and then only occasionally. I suffered a lot of bullying and it really made me sad even though I tried to keep myself to myself and try and do as best I could to achieve at school. I came out of school in May 1986 so nearly 30 years ago, in the eyes of the experts I had no chance of qualifications but boy did I prove them wrong. I got CSEs in English Literature grade 5, English Language grade 5, Social Studies (politics and current affairs) grade 5, Art grade 5; I failed at maths and General Science.

It was soon discovered that I was 'clumsy' in my movement and dexterity, and I was forever falling over and injuring myself. This was later deemed to be eye hand co-ordination difficulties. I had trouble reading and writing, and I still struggle today. A number of people have helped me to get this book to a readable version of my life, I am so grateful to them and I recently turned 45 years old and so I guess I will always struggle to write stuff in a logical way although I did manage to learn to read - at that time the Local Education Authority did not accept Dyslexia or Dyspraxia as conditions, so I received no help. And found out I only had this condition when I was 30 years old, here's a snap shot of my report for you to see below.

Test Scores

I love music, easy going stuff, although if I was stressed I would listen to Beethoven's 5th Symphony at near full blast. I listen to all sorts of music mainly 80s and 90s and the early 2000s - I think towards the end of the 90s the quality of music went downhill. My music tastes were so far ranging from Cher to Queen, and Chas and Dave and songs like superman. When I was not being bullied I would listen only on occasion if I had my favourite song or Top of the Pops was on. There was a great song, Opposites Attract by Paula Abdul with a pop video with cartoon character, in the video it describes and depicts this cartoon character as a very cool customer who at the time is a female singer, the characters in the video are complete opposites, 'odd balls' even, but they come together. That probably is a good way to explain how I tick really, I was brought up to take everyone as they are, and though you meet lots of people who could be described as odd balls, it is just because every human being is different - it would be a bit weird if we were all the same. I sometimes play that song to remind me of the United Nations Conventions and Treaties on disabled people and thing that is in my roots really, that everyone is entitled to equal personal and other human rights.

Chapter 2 **Family**

Mum

Mum

Mum chose for many years to be known as Paula, and she was great my Mum. My Mum was born in Dulwich, South London on the 4th September 1944 and lived with her parents Rose and George, my Nanny and Grandpa.

Mum would be the first to say that she, like so many others, never really made an effort at school, and when she left school she worked in catering at London County Hall near Waterloo, now a hotel. I stayed there recently, it was pretty bad, don't get me started how bad it was, not far from The Oval cricket ground.

With her first marriage she was blessed with Julie my older sister, but not with a happy relationship. Mum re-established her life and retrained as a medical secretary often working in the London teaching hospitals. In 1970 she and some friends went to a dance at the local police section house and that is where she met my Dad Howard. They have been together from that day until February 2008 when we sadly lost my Mum to a long term illness.

In 1971 she gave birth to Simon and Adrian and in 1972 to Robert, two years later the family moved to Derbyshire, and Mum became full time looking after us and caring for us as a family. In the early 1980s after reading an article in the local paper Dad and my Mum became uncle and aunt to Darren, a little boy with a severe learning disability who lived in a home in Mattock, until the Council decided that he should move nearer to his roots.

Mum was diagnosed as having multiple sclerosis in the mid 80s a time of great distress to all the family, and the following two years were a time of confusion and deterioration. However, one-day Mum turned to Dad and said she was fed up being disabled, and if that was the way it was, then she was going to do something with her life. She became involved with the Community 'dial-a-bus' in Chesterfield and attended Chesterfield College to update her clerical skills. Attending College was a shock for the College who were suddenly made very aware of the needs of disabled students. When she had finished her courses and taken the exams she was not prepared to let things rest.

Mum and her beloved dogs

Mum found a job advert for a new post within the Library Service looking to meet the needs of local people who may have difficulties accessing library services. She went along for the interview not really expecting to get the job, but was absolutely delighted to be appointed as a Support Assistant. Dad suddenly found himself with a wife who enjoyed a full time career. Paula later became the lead person in the Services. But her health was beginning to the get the better of her and after a few years she felt that she could no longer manage and retired. Retirement did not suit Mum and she tried to fill her life with activities. She kept going through sheer determination and loved to travel to different parts of the country in the caravan.

She loved dogs her dogs Sophie, Scooby, Beau, Skye and missed them all terribly. She had a new friend Murphy, who would follow her around the house.

Learning that her kidneys were failing, Mum met that head on, determined to manage the difficulties this would pose. Dialysis was never easy for her, and over the last few months, she hid the facts from everyone that her poor health was beginning to have a real effect on her ability to manage. Her strength of will and her determination to beat the impossible was something that her family and friends admired, but in the end the frailty of her physical health could not be overcome by her mental strength - she fought to the very end and at last she was granted the peace that she needed.

Dad has said that he likes to see her sitting in a peaceful place with her mum and dad and her dogs. Mum was very proud of her children and rejoiced in their successes. She would hope that they will continue not to be defeated by problems and to take life by the scruff of it neck and shake it! Mum was an inspiration to those who knew her and her family and friends will miss her.

Adrian

I've dedicated this book to Adrian; we were very close and it is funny as some of my health issues have been very similar. I do miss him greatly and remember what we did and achieve together. Adrian won 285 medals in competitions as a disabled swimmer. He had the opportunity through friendship to speak to some of the top swimmers in the UK that have gone on to succeed in the sport or gone into the media. Below is the Order of Service for the celebration of Adrian's life:

Service of Thanksgiving
for the life of
Adrian John Cramp
1971 - 2015

at
Chesterfield & District
Crematorium at 1.10 p.m. on
Wednesday 9th September 2015

Minister:
Rev Andrew Sails
Donations in memory of Adrian
are invited for Special Olympics GB

Adrian's family wish to thank their friends
for all their messages and kindness

Dad's reflections:

'They are just like little peaches'.

That's how their Grandpa described them to their Grandma. Shortly after Simon, and his identical twin, Adrian, were born, my Father visited them in hospital.

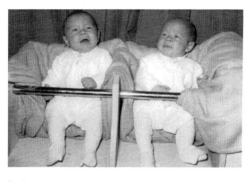

Twins

Simon was born on Sunday, 15th August 1971 at Lambeth Hospital, London. He arrived at 9am and his twin at 9.08am. The twins were induced a month early, because their Mother was struggling to manage. Even their birth was an event. We were asked if we minded some Trainee Doctors and Midwives to be present at the birth, as these needed, as part of their training to see a multiple birth. We were happy for this to happen, especially my wife, who just wanted to have the twins. When the time came we went into what we thought was the delivery room, but in fact was a large room with a lot of trainees. The delivery was very quick, and when they were born they weren't breathing. The Special Care Nursery took charge, and both were helped to start to breathe on their own. Simon was starved of Oxygen for just over a minute. Simon weighed just over 2 bags of sugar, and Adrian just under.

My Father was right they did look like two little peaches. They were both covered in a fine coat of hair.

The twins were discharged from hospital and we took them home. They had to be fed, little and often, in fact every 3 hours. Because they were premature babies they would fall asleep at the drop of a hat and to get them to take their bottle of milk would take over 2 hours, so there wasn't a lot of sleep going off at our house, except for the twins!

I know that Simon has put this book together, and he wanted to tell everyone what it was like to grow up and be Simon, but he is an identical twin, and throughout his life he has been part of a unique and wonderful relationship with Adrian. The twins, as babies and toddlers, were so physically alike it was nearly impossible to tell them apart. Happily Simon liked the colour blue, and Adrian red, so despite liking the same style of clothing, Simon wore it in blue, and Adrian in red. The twins began to show signs that not all was going right, they didn't interact with us properly, living in a little world of their own. They chatted happily to each other, in a language all of their own. We were let into this world very occasionally by being summoned. Mum was Ning and I was Nang. They would call those names and if they called Ning, and Nang arrived, all hell would erupt. Verbal communication with others didn't really start until they were over 3 years old. Simon didn't walk until he was nearly 2 and Adrian until he was over 2. We were just told that they were late developers. Today I really wonder why, no health care professional didn't feel able to tell us that it was very likely that the twins would have a Learning Difficulty. Despite the problems, the twins were well loved by all their family.

Simon and Adrian

We have all heard the stories of the very special relationships, and seemingly uncanny mental linkage, enjoyed by identical twins. Well, I never really believed this, until I became the father to twins. Believe me, it is nearly unbelievable. Simon and Adrian had a relationship that was truly fantastic. They needed to be individuals and would argue and quarrel with each other, but if anyone outside their relationship hurt or insulted one twin then they would have to deal with both twins. If one twin hurt themselves, or was ill, within hours, or even minutes, the other twin would suffer the same injury or illness. This could cause some problems for me, as I was a regular visitor to the local Accident and Emergency Department with one or the other twin. I remember taking Simon down to the hospital, after he had fallen over and cut his forehead wide open. I was taken to one side and seen by the Consultant. He was concerned that my son seemed to be having a lot of injuries. It transpired that he had seen me at the hospital with my son regularly, and the question was, was my son being hurt by me. I explained the situation and this was accepted, thankfully. At this time in my life I was working on the Ambulance Service and one day I got a call to go to my home, where one of my sons needed to go to hospital. Adrian had suffered a hernia and was in a great deal of pain. I took him straight to the hospital, and my wife took Simon round to my parents, before coming to the hospital herself. When the hospital staff realised that I was bringing my own son in, I was allowed to take him straight to the operating theatre. I know that the operation started at 6pm, and later my parents told me that at 6pm, Simon was coming down the stairs and suddenly bent over, clutching his stomach. There was nothing wrong with Simon and this was the first indication we had that the twins were able to feel each other's discomfort, and they soon demonstrated that when they felt the other twin was unwell.

School was not the happiest time for the twins; they just didn't seem to grasp what was happening. Try as they might, school seemed to be a mystery. Unhappily not only did they struggle to learn, they were bullied and teased by the other children because of their difficulties. This sad situation continued throughout school, and must have been very distressing. I recall that on one occasion, on a Friday afternoon, getting a telephone call from the school. It seemed that the main school bully had been targeting Simon for weeks, and at break time, he had knocked Simon to the floor. Instead of getting upset, Simon had reacted aggressively, and had got off the floor and somehow had pushed the bully to the floor, and sat on him punching him repeatedly. School staff had stopped this, and it was necessary for Simon to be taken home. Simon was suspended for the rest of the week, about 1 hour, and the other boy for the whole of the next week. Thankfully Simon did learn that physical violence is not the answer to problems.

The twins did not get any special help with schooling, but were sent for assessment by the Educational Psychologists. This revealed that they were both Dyslexic, a condition not recognised by the Local Education Authority, so no help there then! Mum and I would spend hours each evening doing homework with the boys. We were told that homework would be set, and would take about 20 minutes. Often two to three hours later, we may have just got through, and I know on occasions we did their homework for them.

Upon leaving school, the twins went to the local college, and thinking about it now, I believe that this was the start of Simon beginning to become the person he is today. He began to develop, through work placements, experience of other's needs, a social conscience. He began to develop a view of the world about him, and how everybody is equal, only some are more equal than others, and those who struggle are often left behind. Simon was sent for an assessment by a Clinical Psychologist, and she determined that Simon had a Specific Learning Difficulty, namely Dyspraxia. This means that he has difficulty processing the information that comes to him by sight, by hearing and other forms of delivery. He can't respond quickly and then when explaining himself has to do so in a manner that is very long winded. If interrupted he will start all over again. He is un-coordinated, clumsy and bumps into things and people. I have always told him, jokingly that he would forget his head if it wasn't fixed on. At last someone had, in a word, described the way Simon is and how he understands the world. He does view the world in black and white, knowing what is right and wrong. This can be problematic, as most of the way society operates is in that strange grey area of compromise. Today Simon still has people making obscene and unkind comments to him. Because he is slower, and walks in an uneven line, he does get pushed out of the way by other people. He doesn't understand why this happens, and feels less valuable than others, and that his views are not as worthy as other people's.

Adrian in his element

Adrian had taken a different path in life, he found sport. He was equally awkward and un-coordinated, but he just loved sport. He started to work, on a sheltered employment scheme, for a local council as a Sports Development Worker. Shortly after he started work it was noticed that he couldn't swim. This was rectified by the swimming teachers, and within months Adrian found his niche in life.

Adrian did swim for the East Midlands Team at the UK Special Olympics in 2001 and also represented Great Britain in a swimming gala in Geneva, Switzerland. Plenty of Silver and Bronze medals, but much to his distress no gold! He loved swimming, gaining a swimming teacher's qualification and helping out at special needs swimming events throughout the country.

In 2007, Adrian was on his way to work when he felt unwell; he had suffered a heart attack. Following this his health began to deteriorate and sadly, in 2015, Adrian passed away. Simon did not deal with this well; he had lost his 'other half', his twin. Simon had suffered a heart attack in 2012, and when you think that he had always had the same problems as his twin, he truly believed that he was likely to die soon. I sat with Simon and we talked about our joint loss, and he did understand that life isn't always fair or predictable. He told me that it was not how long we lived, but what you do whilst you live. True!

Simon is who he is, and I am very pleased that he has developed into who he is. I certainly don't understand everything he does, and I am happy for him to explain things to me. I am now his interpreter, as everything he writes, he sends to me for translation into understandable English. It has taken me years to interpret what he writes, and it is very pleasing to note that he thinks of others, rather than concentrating on his needs. I do not know what the book will say, but recommend it as I know it will come from the heart.

I would love to live in a society wherein it is unacceptable for the strong to belittle, bully and pick on the less able, and that we must each of us stand up to those bullies. To look at ways in which to implement the law of the land that can be used to protect the more vulnerable members of our society should not be allowed to take a long time, measures need to be put in place as soon as possible.

The law is there to protect all citizens, but the implementation of how it does so is the key. A number of years ago, children were considered to be poor witnesses and a system was implemented wherein they gave their evidence on video, and were cross questioned about their evidence on that video. They can give evidence on video-links, and Judges, Magistrates and Court Staff are trained to manage the court for these witnesses. Surely it is not too much to suggest that a similar scheme can be used for other vulnerable people.

Dad

Howard Cramp

Well that is what my Dad wrote about me, but he never says anything about himself. That's who he is. He always says he's shy, but he's not really, he just doesn't think anyone would be the slightest bit interested in what he does. He has a Facebook page, but there is nothing on it! My Dad has always tried to be there for his family; he always worked full time and did some of the most emotionally draining jobs around. For nearly 30 years leading up to his retirement, he was a Social Worker in Children's Services, not a 9 – 5 job, and he would work long hours, but would always be there for us all. Around December each year he would always take some time off before Christmas to make sure the shopping was done, he would be dashing about from place to place so that everything would be in place for a lovely family Christmas. However, he always worked the few days before Christmas, and those days could be long. I remember a few Christmas Eves when he would arrive home early, but tired, to find my Mum sitting with her coat on wanting to go to the shops for one thing or another. We could see by his face that this was probably the last thing he wanted to do, but off he went. That's just him; he would always try to meet the needs, and wants of others, before his.

My Dad is also quite stubborn. I have met with quite a few people that worked with him and knew of him. They have said that he knew his job, and that he always worked for the children and families in a positive way, but wasn't frightened of taking whatever action was necessary to protect the children. He wasn't always overly popular with his Managers because he would question their decisions if he thought they were wrong. Somebody once told me that if a Manager said Jump, some would say 'How High', but my Dad would smile, tilt his head and say 'Why'? 'Explain your thinking and decision'. Then if he was instructed to take a course of action he disagreed with, he would ask for that instruction in writing.

After my Mum died, my Dad did everything he could to help us all deal with our distress. I know that Adrian and I took up a lot of his time and he never had time to grieve for his loss. Looking back I can see that he began to lose his spark and drive. Shortly after my Mum died, my Grandma died, my Dad's Mum, and he'd lost two important parts of his life. In 2010 he found himself sitting in his car in a lay-by not

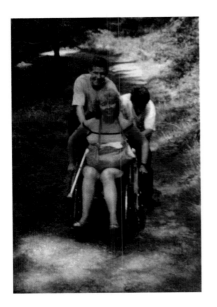

quite understanding how he got where he was. He retired from work in 2011, and he has got on with his life. Adrian's passing shook him, but he's still there for us all.

He will listen to what people say, and will put his point of view. He doesn't believe a word printed in the papers and thinks the words Journalist and Truth should never be used in the same sentence. He believes that life experience is better than any academic degree, and that the belief that 'hands on' public workers need good life experience as well as vocational training.

That's my Dad, for all his faults, he's been there for us.

Chapter 3 **Early Days**

Dad has told the story of my early life and my family life – school, college and first jobs set the scene for my life as a campaigner.

Clowne College

Clowne college

It was great fun, but it was not all fun. Me and other students on my course got looked at funny, not in a good way, because I 'walked funny' and still do today. Overall it was a good learning curve, and was interesting. It was at Clowne College that I got a taste for campaigning and the media. Because of my Mum's diagnosis of multiple sclerosis my brother and I decided we wanted to set up a charity football match. It was great, the Principal of the college, and the head of my course gave their support, the P.E. department were very supportive and we raised a few hundred pounds, it was a great success.

Simon and Adrian: goalful of cash

We made the local paper, the Derbyshire Times and that was my first picture of many that I would have in my life either fighting or campaigning or celebrating my achievements within the media.

Chesterfield College

I did my further education at Chesterfield College, it was similar to Clowne College but it was more structured in that I did more work towards some very meaningful and powerful statements. I then gained a Duke of Edinburgh award in 1989 and also City and Guilds in basic maths, and computers. I was at the time working on and using the famous BBC computer with some of the buttons on the computer different colours which was fun. After that I learned more computer skills, cutting and pasting, how to do PowerPoint and other programmes, the only one I could not get the hang of was Excel spreadsheets, I hate them!

It was during this time at Chesterfield College that I began thinking about how I could use my caring side, build on my campaigning nature and give something back to society.

First Jobs

Upon the completion of my secondary education I did gain a small number of CSEs (Certificate of Secondary Education) at low grades, mainly through the reader and writer scheme. I went to the local college, where they had a Special Needs Department, and I did a number of courses including Sports and Caring. I did a number of work experience placements in the care sector, mainly in homes for older people. It was noted that I had an aptitude for some elements of this type of work, but did struggle with the personal care elements, and with the written work. I did obtain employment as a one-to-one carer for a young man with significant special needs, within the day care situation. I am aware, from supervisors and line managers at the time, that I did a really good job, taking the young man out of a day centre and into community situations safely, giving him a wealth of experiences. The downside

26

was that the man's parent did not agree with much of the programme I was given to perform, and made numerous complaints to senior managers, and the day centre staff would not assist, even to supervise the young man whilst I took a toilet break.

Sadly, the young man passed away, through natural causes, and I was appointed by managers as a Day Services Worker within a Day Centre. The appointment was not welcomed by some other staff and they went out of their way to make life difficult for me and it was later ascertained that I did not receive any professional supervision by my line manager. This situation broke down as unsustainable, and I was transferred to another Centre, dealing with elderly people, but I was totally out of my depth, and by agreement my contract was terminated. All these employments were undertaken under the supported employment scheme and with the local county council.

I saw my career taking a different path and begun to get involved in campaigning work, which has filled my life ever since.

Chapter 4 **Mencap**

With my friend and mentor, Lord Rix

My proud moments are my work of moving through the ranks of Mencap and starting as a volunteer at an elderly person project to moving up to be the person that voted on behalf of all at what was then called Chesterfield Mencap, I then moved on to national Mencap and working my way through the ranks, to be elected to the National Assembly and then Board of Trustees.

I spent a lot of my time at the local Gateway club in Chesterfield it was on Monday and Tuesday and I really enjoyed learning about play and seeing how people with a learning disability had fun. I met Paul Lunn, who then ran the elderly project at the time in about 1988 or 1990; my memory is not as good as it was. I learned all the tricks and how to achieve great things and began to mix with the 'Top Brass' at the Royal Mentally Handicapped Society for Children and Adults as then was. I started to make my mark and grew into the role and started doing media and newspaper and radio interviews.

Also I have a few ex colleagues who give their perspective and insight in the work I did for Mencap. In about 1989 I started looking at getting on to boards for not-for-profit organisations, in the next chapter I will look back on this Mencap work and people who knew me then will give their perspective.

All About Us

Extracts from the book: 1946-2006 The Royal Mencap Society celebrates its 60th year

Perhaps the most significant aspect of the day, though was the seminar chaired by Simon Cramp. In his introductory remarks Simon reminded us a few years ago, as someone with a learning disability (albeit relatively mild,) he would not be allowed such a role, although the occasion was dedicated to the history of people whose label he shares. Simon at that time both a Mencap Trustee and a member of Mencap National Assembly illustrates how much the world has changed. That things have changed so much is a tribute to people such as Simon (who is now a consultant on matters concerned with learning disability) as well as family carers, parliamentarians, professionals, policy makers and Mencap itself. In the 1990s Roger Galletley (then Chairman of Gateway Mencap's leisure arm), Fred Heddell (then Mencap CEO) and I (then Mencap chairman) went on a country-wide tour trying to sell the new, fully inclusive, Mencap constitution to a somewhat doubtful membership. Simon was at one of the meetings and confounded all present by cogently arguing for this change and then informing them that he had a learning disability. Furthermore when the time came to vote on the new constitution at an EGM, Simon made the concluding and I think in many ways the conclusive speech. The new constitution was approved by over 88 per cent of the total vote.

Front cover of *All about us!*

Simon Cramp has been involved with Mencap at a local level in Chesterfield since he was sixteen or seventeen years old, when he was a student at a further education college on a special needs course. He first came to the attention of the Mencap hierarchy when Lord Rix, Roger Galletley ,and Fred Heddell visited the area to debate the proposed constitution changes in 1998 Simon continues the story:

"When I got up to speak and surprised everyone when it was revealed I had a learning disability. This was followed, in October 1998, by the AGM when Lord Rix spoke to me beforehand and

30

said that he was planning to invite me speak – to deploy me as a secret weapon – to persuade people of the need for people with a learning disability to get the chance to become much more involved in strategic decisions about Mencap (i.e. on the national assembly) so I spoke at the end of the debate and told audience that they had to give people with a learning disability a work. This completely changed the mood of the occasion and I think was a key factor in winning the argument..."
After the constitutional change in 2000 Brian Baldock, Mencap Chairman since December 1998, recognised Simon-who by now was serving on the new National Assembly- had exceptional qualities and suggested he might wish to become trustee, if elected Simon writes:

"Then somehow and from somewhere (I'm not sure how or where), the idea started going around that maybe I could even become a trustee. I ummed and ahhed about it a lot, because I wanted to do it, but was worried about the level of commitment I might need to make. But in the end I thought it was too big an opportunity to let go by. When I was elected, it was a great shock and I was delighted."

Simon served the Society well as a trustee for four years before many other outside commitments - all connected with learning disability - made it impossible for him to continue. However he is still a great supporter of Mencap and attends all relevant and important meetings including those held by the All Parliamentary Group on Learning disability.

Leading from the Front

Simon Cramp was the first person with a learning disability to be elected as a trustee. Here he speaks about what it meant to him to have so much involvement in Mencap work, and what he thinks Mencap should learn from his experiences.

"I wanted to put something back into the local community and to help others who were weren't as articulate and clued as me. It wasn't just about personal gratification. It such a fantastic experience and I have learned so much about myself and what you have to do to get things done. In the future, I think Mencap has got to try and get people with a learning disability into top jobs. This has to happen for Mencap to grow and mature. For it to happen there would have to be a lot more support. And I believe that Mencap is really trying to make this happen now."

31

What follows are reflections from some of my old colleagues at Mencap.

Don Derrett worked with Simon at Mencap and together they co-founded Self Direct. Don writes:

It was a hot day and the gentle breeze blew in the fragrance of freshly mowed grass through the open office window. As I raised the mug to my lips the coffee was cold and bitter on my tongue but this was nothing new; urgent and unexpected activity in the residential home was often followed later by a moment of quiet reflection over a mug of cold coffee. My coffee in one hand and a copy of the Mencap in house journal in my other, it was a moment to catch my metaphorical breath. A picture in the magazine caught my eye and it brought back memories of a very different day 2 months earlier. The people in the photo were clapping and cheering and in the middle of this throng, on the front row, was a young man standing with his arms raised aloft, fists clenched and with an expression of utter triumph and joy on his face; that young man was Simon Cramp.

That year, an historic decision had been taken to include people with a learning disability in the governance of Mencap. It had been a difficult campaign to try to convince the members of Mencap at that time to vote in favour of this big change to Mencap's constitution. The members were small in number and included a big proportion of die-hard old fashioned carers, many of whom couldn't imagine their son or daughter being able to make decisions about their own lives, never mind decisions about such a large and complex organisation as Mencap. However, luckily for Mencap at that time they had a visionary Chair in Lord Rix, who led the way in campaigning for the change to the constitution and also luckily for Mencap, there were people with a learning disability like Simon, who knew how to get their voices heard.

Later in 2014 when Lord Rix was 90, to mark his achievement of reaching that veritable age, he was asked to reflect on his time supporting the work of Mencap. He was quoted on Mencap's website as saying that the charity's decision to change its constitution in 1998 to include people with a learning disability ranked amongst its finest moments. Simon and I were both at the Mencap Annual Conference in 1998, when the vote for this momentous change was taken. We didn't know each other then and we didn't meet on that day; it seems strange now to think of how later that same year our lives would start to become intertwined.

As I looked at the photo on that hot day in the office, the memories of the day at the Conference flooded back. It was an exciting time; you could feel the energy throughout the conference venue, people were buzzing with anticipation as the moment of the result of the vote approached. I had left the hall for a moment to take a minute to reflect and have a hot cup of coffee. I was sitting quietly thinking at a table just a short distance from the main conference hall when suddenly the result was announced in favour of the change. I stood up quickly as I heard a tremendous roar of approval in the conference hall; people started pouring out of the hall contacting their family and friends on their mobiles as they rushed down the corridors, telling people, like me, that they met as they went along their way the result of the vote. As I entered the hall it was like the moment immediately after a tremendous storm, the same freshness of that moment filled the air and was mixed with relief, exuberance and smiles of sheer delight on everyone's face. Of course, this was just the start of the major change in the governance of Mencap. Following that day, the plan to put the result into action in a meaningful way had to be created and implemented.

Mencap decided to build a framework of Regional District Committees where people with a learning disability could take a real part in the decision making process. A new membership programme was to be put in place and nominated members would be voted onto the District Committees and the National Assembly by the other members. The role of the Mencap District Officer would change; this included playing a significant part in making those changes happen. Simon became a District Committee member, the National Assembly representative for the East Midlands and a Mencap Trustee.

As I looked at the photo of Simon in the office on that hot day in 1998, I was inspired to meet with him to find out what the changes really meant for people with a learning disability. I decided that I needed to meet Simon in order to get some first-hand insight into what this change meant and Simon agreed to meet me in Chesterfield. I met Simon at a centre for people with a learning disability in Chesterfield. It reminded me of other centres I had visited; there was a distinctive smell in the air, it felt sterile and uninviting and I had the same feeling of unease as I had had in those other places where people with a learning disability were segregated from the rest of society. But as Simon entered the corridor where

I was waiting for him something changed, the energy in the room was transformed, he seemed to light up the corridor with his smile and jaunty walk and I was instantly impressed with his enthusiasm and steely character. He was and still is a charismatic personality, with all the hallmarks of a leader. He was, as always, very generous with his time when we met up for that first time. We discussed many issues; he listened carefully to me and answered all my questions thoughtfully and with great insight. With his guidance, advice and encouragement I knew I had made the right decision to apply for the role of District Officer. Subsequently, I became the District Officer for York and North Yorkshire.

Simon and I stayed in touch during those important years and I found in Simon, someone whose opinion and advice I could respect, trust and use in my work. Simon proved to be a leading light in those changes and spoke passionately about them at conferences and meetings across the UK; inspiring others with his dedication to the cause and utter determination to make the changes work.

During those years, I also worked with Di Lofthouse MBE. Di was a member of the District Committee for York and North Yorkshire and a close friend of Simon. She was the first person with a learning disability to be allowed to attend meetings of Mencap's National Council, the governing body that was replaced by the National Assembly. The National Council was a group of people who were members of Mencap under the old system of governance and it mainly consisted of carers. Di was told she could attend their meetings but she wouldn't be allowed to talk; of course they changed their minds later and eventually Di was allowed to speak at their meetings. Anyone who knows Di will understand why they changed their minds. She, like Simon, is not a person who is willing to accept this kind of behaviour towards people with a learning disability and she, like Simon, is more than capable of standing up for herself and saying with conviction and unwavering principles exactly what is on her mind! Simon and Di were both pioneers in changing attitudes towards people with a learning disability. I found in them both a source of energy and inspiration that helped me keep a real perspective during my time at Mencap.

In 2004 I was appointed by Jo Williams, CEO of Mencap, to support her and the Directors to put Mencap's new strategic plan into action.

I decided that in order to make sure that the work in my new role was meaningful for people with a learning disability; I would consult with and seek advice from Simon and Di. Simon continued to be my mentor throughout those important times for Mencap. And once again, I found that listening to Simon helped me to keep focused on the real purpose of Mencap's work; making sure that the voice of people with a learning disability was heard, listened to and acted upon. The following year, Jo Williams asked me to combine this new role with another, that of supporting the development of a fledgling organisation called In Control. Mencap acted as a 'home' for In Control in its early years and my job as In Control's business manager was to ensure that everything possible was done to support its development.

By 2007 it was evident that In Control was successfully influencing local and national government to make the changes necessary to put self-directed support into action and the changes were happening at an increasingly quickening pace. But it was also becoming clear to me that organisations providing support, like Mencap, were not changing at the same rate. They were being left behind and there was a real danger that practice would not follow the policy changes; I felt something needed to be done and fast.

Mencap was in no position to take on that task; they were already heavily involved in supporting In Control and were themselves working hard to start to make the changes necessary to implement self-directed support across their services and this was proving challenging enough in itself. And although In Control had started to do some work with providers of services, they were already stretched to keep up with the increasing demand to work with practically all the Local Authorities across England. So, I decided I needed to do something about this. But this was a big task and a big step for me personally; it would mean leaving Mencap in order to do it. I had lots of ideas about how to set about this task but I needed to check them out with people I knew and trusted and I also knew I couldn't do it alone.

The first person I called was Simon. I simply said I had something important I needed to talk to him about and I wanted to meet up with him in person to discuss it. Simon was intrigued and we met in the autumn of 2007. I told Simon about these ideas briefly. I told him that it would be necessary for me to leave Mencap and to set up a social enterprise to put these ideas into action and I wanted him to join me in this new initiative. His advice to me was that we should have a meeting with a few others to discuss these ideas more before deciding the next step. Simon suggested we invite Caroline Tomlinson to the meeting. Caroline and I were colleagues at In Control and I knew her innovative, imaginative but also very pragmatic way of thinking, so I agreed to ask her.

Then Simon said we should ask Keith Wyatt to facilitate the meeting for us. I'd worked with Keith on a project to develop and deliver training that would prepare people in the North East of England for the introduction of Learning Disability Partnership Boards; these were set up in each local authority as part of the Government's White Paper, *Valuing People* (2001). Because of the success of this project and other pieces of work that Keith and I had worked on together, I knew Keith was an excellent facilitator. And finally Simon asked if Jackie Lawley could come to the meeting to support him. I didn't know Jackie at that time; she supported Simon and was also a commissioner for a local authority in the Midlands. I trusted Simon's judgment and if she had been chosen by him then I knew she would be a good person to have at the meeting. So, naturally I agreed and the five of us met in York in December 2007.

It was a cold, dark and wet day in York. The uneven pavement slabs were slippery underfoot as I made my way quickly to the small church room that I had booked for our meeting in the centre of town. As I approached St Wilfrid's Church I looked ahead at the majestic northern entrance of York Minster and felt a sudden nervousness about what was going to happen in the upper room of St Wilfrid's. The room was small, warm and welcoming; the others arrived and we greeted each other. I began to feel completely at ease with Simon, Jackie, Keith and Caroline all now ready to listen to what I had to say.

I started the meeting by outlining some of my ideas. I was expecting Keith to step in and take up his role as facilitator but he wanted me to continue presenting my ideas in more detail and just sat there listening to me, as did the others. When I had finished Keith said "I'm in". It wasn't what I was expecting but it was a great surprise. Then Jackie said "me too", which was also unexpected but welcome. Then I was left waiting with nervous anticipation for Simon to say something. Eventually after giving it some thought he agreed to join us and the four of us became the co-founders of Self Direct.

Simon was inspirational as a director of Self Direct and I felt he was the heart of the organisation. Self Direct started holding training workshops for providers of services in 2008. The aims of the workshops were to explore together the implications for providers of implementing the 7 ethical principles of self-directed support.

I believed and continue to believe that the best people to train providers of support are people who have real life experience of using support. This belief was a key standard underpinning all our work at Self Direct. Therefore, working with Simon to develop Self Direct's work from the very beginning was essential to ensure the organisation could put its words into action. Self Direct's associates had this real life experience and worked alongside other Self Direct team members, social and health care professionals, as equal partners when delivering training together. We agreed that everyone should be paid at the same rate; this was one practical way of demonstrating our values were not just words but that we really were turning our values into action.

Simon was responsible for recruiting many of Self Direct's associates and was also himself a trainer at some of Self Direct's events. Simon and I worked closely together on many of Self Direct's activities and his authoritative voice helped to give Self Direct the integrity necessary to make an immediate impact in the social and health care sector. I'm convinced that it was due to the respect in which Simon is held within government department circles that Self Direct's work with providers came to the attention of the Department for Health. Subsequently, the Department for Health team working on the development of Personal Health Budgets at that time asked if they could join one of the Self Direct events for providers in London. They wanted to discover what Self Direct was doing to prepare providers of services for the changes that would be happening soon following their work in developing Personal Health Budgets. They also wanted to inform providers about this work and to seek feedback.

The work that we did at Self Direct with providers was written up in our first book *Helping Providers to Change*. This book is a useful toolkit of practical ideas for providers of services. Throughout the five years that Self Direct operated, Simon continued to be a passionate and tireless ambassador for the organisation. His influence in various circles across the social and health care sector led to invitations to present Self Direct's work at various conferences in the UK. Simon and I also had a joint article published in Learning Disability Today. The article was our personal review of the *Care and Support White Paper* (2012) and was entitled *Watching Brief*. In the article we expressed our opinion and concerns that although there were many things that were good about the white paper, many of the major issues facing disabled people were not addressed in the white paper.

In 2013 Self Direct's second book, *Self-Direction: The Key to a Better Life*, was published. This book introduces the work of Self Direct and self-directed support. There is guidance on areas to avoid and areas to improve when supporting someone to take control of their life and an outline of the practical implications of putting self-directed support into practice. The main focus is on success stories from Self Direct members, which show how people's lives dramatically improve when the core principles of self-directed support are put into practice. It includes the seven principles of self-directed Support: independent living, entitlement, self-determination, openness, flexibility, learning and contribution and how these seven principles can be used to assess whether people are being supported to achieve self-direction in their lives. The book was published by Pavilion in 2013 and is available to purchase on their website.

Simon was central to getting this second book published; he played an important role in promoting Self Direct to key people at Pavilion. I was able to witness this smooth operator in action at the Learning Disability Today conference in 2012 as he used his considerable powers of persuasion to pave the way for the discussions I had with Pavilion that led to the publication of our second book. By 2013 there were Self Direct members in every region of England and in Wales; between them they were supporting over 110,000 people to take control of their lives by applying the principles of self-directed support.

In 2008, Self Direct had been a pioneer in this area of work; working with providers in a new and innovative way. But by 2013 many other people and organisations had entered this area of the social and health care marketplace and were providing similar training. In the five years Self Direct was operating we had achieved our main objective; to stimulate changes in the social and health care marketplace so that people who needed support would be supported to take control of their lives. Of course after 2013 many organisations continued to push forward with this work. This was in spite of the Government's austerity agenda, which has had a massive negative impact on this work and at the time of writing has the potential to reverse many of the important changes we were able to achieve with others working in this field.

In the early years of Self Direct, Simon and I worked together as part of the leadership team to make these changes happen. And when he chose to step down as a director because of other pressures in his life, he continued to promote Self Direct and to be my mentor and guide. During that time, we would often meet up in Chesterfield in a pub or restaurant to share a meal and catch up on each other's news. I was always amazed and continue to be amazed at the number and variety of causes across the social and health care sector, and further afield, that Simon gets involved in and influences one way or another.

When Simon and I used to meet up, I imagined I was like a gold prospector! Imagine the scene, Simon and I sitting in a cosy pub in Chesterfield, greeted warmly by the landlady. He and I drinking and eating the local fare, good pub grub. We would be talking away, often about subjects of no particular importance or of interest to others but always interesting to me none the less. Then suddenly, there it was, coming out of his mouth, a 'nugget of gold'! Pure insight, pure inspiration and 'nuggets of gold' about how to improve life for people with a learning disability, and believe me those 'nuggets of gold' were always worth waiting for!

And what's even more amazing to me, is that he has often continued with his quest to improve life for people with a learning disability even when he has been in very poor health from time to time. He seems unstoppable and is a constant inspiration to me and to many others I'm sure.

In 2013 I moved to France for personal reasons but since then, Simon and I have kept in touch. Also, I regularly follow Simon's postings on Facebook and find his postings an invaluable way to keep abreast of what is really happening in the UK for disabled people. This year, two of my friends from England visited me in France. They are health and social care sector professionals, qualified social workers with vast and extensive knowledge and years of experience. I told them that I followed events in the UK through Facebook and asked them if things were really as bad for disabled people in England as they seemed to be from the postings I read on Facebook. With extreme gravity they confirmed that sadly, it was all too true and they recounted some real life stories of people known to them who had paid the ultimate price for the Government's cut backs and had died.

Simon and I continue to be connected professionally; we are both fellows of the Centre for Welfare Reform. As a consequence of the present Government's cut backs, the Centre for Welfare Reform has become a campaigning organisation; fighting against the Government's austerity policies that have targeted disabled people disproportionately more than the rest of the population.

When Simon and I were working together at Self Direct, many of the delegates at our events used to say that self-directed support offered a fantastic opportunity to improve the lives of disabled people but often asked the question: what would happen if and when there was a change of government? No one could have predicted that the change in government in 2010 could have led to such devastating consequences for disabled people in the UK.

Now and the future, I know I can rely on Simon's postings and comments on Facebook to give me a true picture of the situation in the UK. Simon continues in his quest to improve the lives of people with a learning disability and is a constant source of encouragement to keep up the fight to achieve social justice for disabled people.

I want to give Simon the last word in my contribution to his book. Below is the Foreword to our book *Self-Direction: The Key to a Better Life*. This was written by Simon and reproduced here with the kind permission of Pavilion Publications.

Most people take freedom and, as a result, personalisation as a given. But for someone with a learning disability, or any other disability, that is not always the case. This means that there are often more controls and fewer choices in their lives. As a result, people can miss out on some of the most important things in life.

A lot has happened in my life. I have a learning disability, but I am passionate about politics and the rights of people with learning disabilities. I bought my first newspaper when I was 14 years old – The Guardian. I often went without my lunch so I could afford it and I would rush out of school to go and buy it. I have kept trying to contribute and give something back to the community, and to stick up for people like me and others who have even more severe disabilities. For many years people with learning disabilities and their allies have been campaigning for the right for people to have more control over their own lives. In response to this, in England the Government published a consultation document.

In 2003 Parliament set up a joint committee to review the draft legislation on mental capacity, which at the time was the Mental Incapacity Bill. I wrote to the committee, with the support of Mencap, and was invited to speak to the committee at the Palace of Westminster. It was a nerve-wracking experience, but I was able to argue that people should have a clear right to advocacy and that there should be better safeguards for people with severe disabilities. Some important changes were made to the final legislation. I was very proud to be one of the first people with learning disabilities ever to speak to a committee in Westminster.

Then, in 2005, I worked with Simon Duffy to publish an important paper on self-determination and individual budgets. We explained how it was possible for people with learning disabilities to control their lives, including any budget for their support. I have been lucky. I was given the chance to exercise control and be in control of my own life. There have been many low points, and many plus points, but I was very lucky to have had good parents and the support of friends and family. But some people are not so lucky.

I hope and pray that one day everyone – whether or not they have a learning disability or any other disability – will have freedom. Choice and control should be a given. We should not have to keep fighting for our freedom.

David Congdon, former Head of Campaigns and Public Policy at Mencap writes:

I joined Mencap in 1998 a few months before the historic vote to change its constitution to have people with a learning disability on its National Assembly. Prior to the vote there was lot of nervousness as to whether members would support this change. The game changer was Simon's speech at the Extraordinary General Meeting in Bournemouth. The euphoria on winning the vote was fantastic and provided a good foundation for the work ahead.

My experience had been mainly in political campaigning, I had no background in working with people with a learning disability. I soon got to know Lloyd Page and others working in the office. Then Simon started to thrive on the National Assembly and perhaps more significantly on the Board of Trustees. Simon would often pop into the office to discuss campaigning issues. He also provided valuable input into our work.

It is hard to remember the wide range of issues and problems we discussed. But he was particularly passionate about the work on the Mental Capacity Bill and all aspects of disability rights. He certainly helped the campaign team get a deep insight of the concerns of people with a learning disability.

I do recall Simon's help in encouraging us to persevere with our work on health. *Treat Me Right* had been a great report but had limited impact. Subsequent to producing this report, we were working on dreadful cases of people dying unnecessarily at the hands of the NHS. He was one of those who encouraged us to publish what became known as *Death by Indifference*. This was the most influential report that Mencap ever produced. Its tragic case studies could not be ignored. Those with profound disabilities were the ones usually at most risk of dying in hospital, and Simon was always interested in ensuring we campaigned for a better deal for them in all aspects of their life.

Simon fought hard to force government departments to produce easy read versions of White Papers and other reports. He also challenged them over their failure to make printed copies of reports available to the public. He would often turn up in my office with carrier bags full of the latest reports. He had browbeaten officials into submission often by claiming he was a press reporter! What a great campaigner.

I thoroughly enjoyed my discussions with Simon. Even though we had a somewhat different political perspective, we never fell out. Our common aim was to fight for equal rights for disabled people and encourage all of Mencap to do more campaigning. I also saw Simon in action at Trustee meetings. He was rightly challenging but always with good humour and courtesy. It was great having a friend at court.

Simon's campaigning and influence on various committees was also an inspiration to other people with a learning disability. They saw what could be achieved in part thanks to the work of Simon; people with learning disability now have a real voice. Yes, there is more to do, but without the inspiration of Simon, people with a learning disability would still be out of sight, and out of mind. We would still be a long way from people with a learning disability being listened to.

Beverley Dawkins, CEO Generate writes:

I met Simon when I joined Mencap in January 2000 as National Officer for people with profound and multiple learning disabilities. During this time Simon became one of Mencap's trustees, I believe he was the first person with a learning disability to join the board. I am sure that he must have been selected for this important role because of the keen interest that he has always shown in fighting for the rights of people with a learning disability. Simon was a regular visitor to the campaign and policy department while he was a trustee and would often call in to collect the latest draft of a government consultation or policy document and to discuss the Mencap response with the team.

Simon has always been a fantastic networker. Over the years I am certain that he will have made contact with literally anyone who was anyone in the learning disability sector. He has always been willing to facilitate introductions and share information across the network that he has built up.

One of the pieces of work that Simon and I did together while we were both at Mencap that especially stands out, is when he joined the steering group for the Multi Media Project that I had set up. Nowadays the idea of using film and photography to support people with profound and multiple learning disabilities in communicating what is important about their lives and how best to support them is pretty much standard. But back then it was innovative and indeed some people were sceptical of its potential benefit. But not Simon, he became a champion of the approach and gave all the Mencap staff involved in the work his full support. With Simon's involvement in the project we also had a positive voice, speaking up for people with profound and multiple learning disabilities on the Mencap board and beyond.

Simon has always been a great support to me in my work but I also think of him as a great friend well it has been 15 years Simon! When fairly new in my role as CEO of Generate, I was delighted when one of the team put through a call saying, 'there's a guy called Simon Cramp on the phone for you- do you know him?' Well of course I did and was so pleased that we have continued to stay in contact, share our knowledge and information and just as importantly, lend each other a little support in the good times and the not so good times! Here's to the next 15 years Simon!

Chapter 5 **Dimensions**

Well I first came across Dimensions when it was known as New Era Housing. I understand it was associated with the Royal Mencap Society as its housing arm. I got to know the business as I did my research because they were advertising for board members and I thought, 'why not apply for it, see what happens'. This was in 1999 and after filling in the application I was invited to a day to meet the senior management, and also have an interview with senior members of the board and the chief executive to see if I was suitable.

Lucky I was, and I started work with this group. The board came from all different backgrounds finance people, people with a learning disability with real life experience of having a disability and knowing what it was like, people who knew about the finance and others including human resources. And I was so pleased that I was part of this great team. But I served on this group who deal with housing for people with a learning disability, and helping them to become independent in their own home with support. As the board we gave the leadership of the organisation by setting budgets and plans and highlighting the senior directors of the organisation but also having to make the very difficult decisions like letting people go and also being part of some very tough decisions and periods of being a director when in the early 2000s we had some problems. I was also a trustee with a rival of Dimensions UK as it then was; at times very difficult but I can't say I was a lawyer in disguise! What was important: I read the relevant and other Acts and government policy that was current and critical to do the best job I could i.e. the Companies Act 2006 and the Industrial and Provident Society Act 1971 and it was difficult.

You build up relationships with people in difficult times and one such was David Wolverson. David is great at networking, encouraging me to better myself but also respectful of my talents to make the world better but would also give me honest advice. I got on with the senior management David Wolverson CEO, Steve Scown -Head of Marketing and Business Development, Andy Donelan - Head of Human Resources and Kevin Fairman - Finance Director. Kevin was the best at giving the figures of how much money we had in simple language – in the next breath he'd talk to an accountant on the board in accountant speak! As a member of the board we would integrate and take part and get to know each other in the context of making a difference to the lives of people with learning disability.

I was on the board for 9 years, the organisation would let you sit on for only 9 years then you had to leave, it was a good way for the company to help keep bringing in new people and fresh blood and new ideas and in some cases a new direction of hitting that goal of implementing the reality of *Valuing People* and its values and principles. But before I left, David Wolverson spent some of his time helping me look at other options about what to do next after Dimensions.

Here are some reflections from some of my old colleagues at Dimensions.

Linda Russell Ward, Involvment Co-ordinator, Dimensions writes:

I have known Simon Cramp for 15 years. We first met at a New Era (now called Dimensions) Board of Management meeting in London. I had just started a new job as personal assistant and was attending my first meeting to take the minutes which in itself was a bit of a daunting task; to meet a room full of strangers and do my best to catch all that was said and hope that I would capture a correct record of the meeting for this formal gathering – thankfully I needn't have worried!

Simon was a non-executive member and straight after the meeting he came over and introduced himself and instantly I felt a 'northern welcome' and his cheerful disposition. Simon retained his position on the Board for a number of years contributing his breadth of knowledge to very meaningful discussions and behaving always in a respectful, professional manner. Simon is a great ambassador and champions the views of the learning disability sector in a powerful way sharing from his own personal experience and unafraid to challenge and speak out when something is not right.

During this time we spent long hours on the train together travelling down and back to London and we got to know each other fairly well. He was always a great support to me and a real gentleman, carrying my laptop as well as his own, plus another heavy bag full of papers on the latest Government White Papers and policy documents – Simon seemed to be a mind full of information and relished in these things!

When Simon's term of office came to stand down from the Board he was employed by Dimensions as a Learning Disability Advisor. It's fair to say – and Simon would agree – he struggled with this role. Not, I hasten to add that he didn't know his stuff, far from it, but he didn't find it easy to put his thoughts down in writing and the job became too stressful. After exhausting the merits of Access to Work a very amicable decision was made and Simon decided to move on.

That was 5 years ago and it's to Simon's credit and his character he has kept in touch with many of his work colleagues and the friendships he made have continued. I am aware of some difficult health issues that Simon has been facing, but I sincerely wish him good health and happiness. I always imagined I'd see Simon on the telly one day on BBC Question Time or something similar – and still wouldn't rule that out – he has a real gift and shows a sensitive, but authoritative manner. In all this I have found Simon to be truly inspirational and he certainly has had his voice heard in campaigning and advocating for the rights of people with learning disabilities.

David Wolverson, former CEO of Dimensions writes:

My first encounters with Simon were, auspiciously, just before the Millennium.

At the time I was Chief Executive of New Era Housing Association. Whilst my professional background had very limited contact with people with learning difficulties, I knew I wanted New Era's Board to have more direct contact with the people they served. It was Simon's name that came into the frame!

At the time he was known for his work at Mencap where he was a member of the local society as well as being a Trustee on the main Board. This was a good fit for New Era as many of our houses were managed by either Royal Mencap or local Mencap societies.

Over the years, Simon's background story gradually emerged. He does not wear his heart on his sleeve, but someone nosey like me can dig a little. The more I dug the more I understood the obstacles that people, like Simon, have to overcome. Often people with learning difficulties have other physical and developmental conditions, and the society heaps a load more problems upon them because we do not adapt to allow people to live like others in their communities. When you take even one step in Simon's shoes, I wondered how he had not become an angry young man. His attitude was very much this is the stuff that happens to you when you have a disability; don't dwell on it but go and do something positive to make change happen for people with disabilities. He is such a shining light of positivity!

47

Simon's other impressive skill is his serial networking. No one is safe from Simon's advances! The great and the good, the commentators in the national newspapers, the policymakers in Whitehall, the leaders in the pressure groups but also staff and most importantly other people with learning disabilities. Watching Simon at the National Social Services conferences was a 'masterclass' in how to network; refreshing his contacts, making new connections and wheedling himself into receiving pre-public releases of Whitehall policy documents!

Simon took time to read these documents (whilst others like me waited for summaries) and he would often remind the Dimensions Board in its deliberations about latest government thinking; challenging them and the Executive into considering what needs to change. He would go on to raise questions about the impact of these policies on the people we supported and the way Dimensions worked in trying to put people in control of their lives.

As I write this piece, I can reflect on the influence Simon has had on Dimensions, other organisations and me. He did it without me really appreciating at the time the depth of what he was doing. A truly warm and generous man.

Gordon Stephens, Learning Consultant at Dimensions writes:

I first became aware of Simon and the role he had on the Board of New Era Housing Association, while I was a team manager at a service in Sheffield. During this time Simon worked tirelessly to give a voice to the people we support.

My working relationship with Simon developed in 2004 when I was seconded to a project, on which Simon was chairperson. Simon chaired the meetings with authority ensuring that everyone had the opportunity to raise questions and ensured answers were given or sought. Our relationship continued throughout the project during which time I admired Simon's perspective on how the project we were working would apply to people with learning disabilities.

Simon has a vast wealth of working knowledge of applicable laws and Acts of Parliament that I find useful and enjoyable as I find Simon an excellent sounding board for ideas and resources. I feel privileged to be able to call Simon a friend, whom I can always rely on to be open, honest and truthful with his answers.

Steve Scown, CEO Dimensions, writes:

I've known Simon for over 16 years and for most of those worked closely with him in a variety of ways. Simon is one of those people you're glad you've met because they have left lasting impressions in how you look at things that have shaped and influenced your thinking. Simon is someone who cares about other people and even when he was going through tough times at home and with his own health he was invariably interested in how you were and whether he could do anything to help you. Throughout I have always found Simon's demeanour to be one of positivity. Apart from politicians of a certain hue I cannot recall him ever having a bad word to say about anyone. Even when frustrated about how his local social services were helping him and his family – or rather how he felt they were not – Simon consistently recognised it was the system and not the individuals working within it that was the problem.

Whether as a travelling companion on so many train journeys between Chesterfield and London, or as a Dimensions Board member or as our Learning Disability Advisor I never found Simon to be shy in making his views known. As someone who doesn't enjoy the reading of lengthy government publications, on more occasions than I should perhaps acknowledge, Simon came to my rescue. His determination to understand the government's intention and to then think through its potential impact on people with learning disabilities was something I not only greatly admired, but also on many occasions gratefully benefitted from.

Simon has consistently fulfilled a powerful ambassadorial role for people with learning disabilities. His opinion has been welcomed by many people and his perspective has shaped many people's thinking and positions. Whilst not explicitly drawing upon his own experiences as a person with a learning disability invariably this helped establish his credentials and so make his voice one that has been listened to.

Inevitably our conversations usually focused on the rights of people with learning disabilities and the justice and fairness (or not) of central government policy. Occasionally however, we allowed ourselves to drift onto conversations about the latest England sporting performance – be it rugby, football or cricket. In addition to recalling his warmth and keenness to discuss and debate almost anything I have been prompted to remember Simon's sense of humour. Whether dishing it out or on the receiving end so many of our conversations ended with a shared laugh.

Chapter 6 National Policy

I've always been interested in politics and policy and over the years I have had the chance to get involved in lots of important policy developments.

Valuing People

Around the time I was at Mencap and Dimensions, the White Paper *Valuing People* was being implemented.

Valuing People had 4 key principles;

1. Rights
2. Independence
3. Choice
4. Inclusion

And a lot key targets, It covered the areas of Health, Education, Employment and Housing.

There were targets for improving people's health, housing plans and employment and how to get more people with a learning disability into employment where the figures at the time were only 7 per cent 10 per cent at the most.

There was a structure of local partnership boards and there was also a start up fund to support the new National Forum and I was one of the founder members. As Mencap we were tasked to help set up the systems to make sure that what the White Paper wanted to achieve was made possible. The National Forum was set up to do this; after the initial period there would be two people to be elected from each region In England, and also a link direct to the Department for Health by having two representatives from the National Forum to sit also on the new group called the *Learning Disability Task Force*. This Task Force had chief executive experts and Department for Health representatives who made decisions and gave advice to ministers in the Blair Government.

I was involved with setting up the National Forum; here are some reflections from my colleague, John Hersov.

John Hersov, Freelance Consultant writes:

Simon Cramp and I first worked together in the original line up of the National Forum during the early *Valuing People* days. I don't think our paths had crossed before then, but it was clear from the outset that Simon had a particular interest in identifying the connection between the personal and the political.

This set him apart from a lot of other people for whom speaking up for themselves was what they wanted to do – as an end in itself if you like. Simon was keen to see how he and others could influence people with political power to change the ways they dealt with people with learning disabilities. Not an easy task, but one which suited his brand of dogged cussedness.

I have learnt more about Simon's work since that time from other people's testimonies in this book. We had not linked up for quite a while when I was pleased to hear that he would be chairing the session at the Learning Disability Today London 2016 event in which I was going to talk about my work co-ordinating Transport for London's (TfL) Valuing People Big Day Network over the last 10 years.

He did a good job keeping all the speakers to task at the end of a long day with his humour intact, always a challenge but one he handled with good grace. Liaising about this event gave us the chance to re-connect and I sense that this time we will keep it going. Simon knows about a lot of things that I don't and I hope that I have some insights that he finds useful. Plus he is the only person in my life who calls me "Young Man", and you can't say fairer than that!

I remember when the updated version of *Valuing People Now* came out in January 2009, and that was for me the tipping point of starting what really should have started in 2001 with a big bang of user participation. I think that should have started over 30 years ago, but instead it was in the early 90s when we started to change government language to get them to think of as someone who has, in the Department for Education wording, a 'learning difficulty' and, in the Department for Health version, a 'learning disability'. The Prime Minister at the time decided that learning disability and autism were going to be the universal descriptions of the condition in general terms and that there were differences in the White Paper for people with other conditions besides learning disability or autism. I think it was when I first started some of my roles in Mencap at a national level and with Dimensions that I got the bug of really wanting to work hard to make a difference, I'm proud of my campaigning work and as well as *Valuing People* I have contributed to a range of National bodies.

Ofcom

I was appointed to Ofcom's advisory committee on older and disabled people in 2004, to make sure that people with a learning disability were not left behind as technology changed. Here's my entry;

> Simon Cramp is a freelance consultant in advocacy and social justice issues for people with learning disabilities. He is a Board member of Dimensions UK, a leading learning disability support provider. He is also a member of the Royal Society of Medicine's forum for learning disability and a fellow of the Royal Society of Arts. Simon is co founder of SelfDirect, a social enterprise scheme looking at how self directed support can play a part in social care

Graham Howell, Secretary to the Corporation writes:

The Office of Communications ('Ofcom') is the regulator for the communications and postal sectors in the United Kingdom. Its purpose is to ensure that all consumers and citizens are well served by telephony, broadband, television, radio and post. Ofcom has a specific remit to ensure that disabled citizens and consumers are able to access all these services. Ofcom has established a Committee specifically to ensure that it is advised appropriately on disabled issues. Simon Cramp was a founding member of the Committee and served it with considerable skill and credit for several years. Simon provided much advice on the disabled community and his input into the Committee's work was invaluable. He was a source of calm, considered and knowledgeable advice which was always well thought through and well received. When Simon retired from the Committee he was very much missed.

The Care Quality Commission

David Behan, CEO CQC writes:

Simon has been a campaigner and advocate for learning disability rights for many years. He brings a perspective of a person who uses services and uses his voice and abilities to represent those without a voice. He is a great networker and uses this network to shape and influence policy at a local and national level. He is always positive and constructive in his approach suggesting what should be done to improve services not just what is currently wrong with them. Along with others Simon has contributed to improving the lives of many through his campaigning and advocacy. He has been a pleasure and a joy to work with.

The Mental Capacity Act 2005

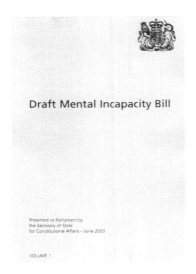

Draft Mental Incapacity Bill

Presented to Parliament by
the Secretary of State
for Constitutional Affairs – June 2003

VOLUME 1

Mental Capacity Bill

This was one of my key areas of policy I love to get stuck into and I hope make a big contribution, but don't take my word for it ask someone who is expert in his field he takes the story up.

Toby Williamson, Head of Development & Later Life, Mental Health Foundation, July 2015 writes:

The proper involvement of people with lived experience of disabilities is an essential part of developing laws and policies that affect their lives. This has often been a hard fought struggle and continues to be something which requires determination, commitment, an understanding of the issues and processes involved, and sometimes a pretty tough skin. There's also a responsibility on organisations and individuals to ensure they make the issues and processes meaningful and accessible to people with disabilities who they involve. The development of the *Mental Capacity Act 2005* posed particular challenges for the meaningful involvement of people with disabilities because the disabilities that affected their mental capacity were often very severe. But this certainly didn't make it impossible and Simon Cramp stands tall as a person with disabilities who made an enormous contribution to that important legislation.

Between 2004 and 2005 I co-chaired the Making Decisions Alliance, a coalition of national and regional disability and older people's charities, which campaigned in support of mental capacity legislation. This was where I first met Simon. Simon gave evidence to a pre-legislative Parliamentary scrutiny committee that looked at the draft *Mental Incapacity Bill* before it began its formal passage through Parliament. Simon's views about the Bill therefore helped shape it, including the legislation being more positively renamed so the Act no longer referred to people's lack of capacity.

But once the Act was passed by Parliament some people might have stopped there, thinking the job was done. Not so Simon. Prior to the Act coming into force in 2007 I worked at the Ministry of Justice to help engage and communicate with key stakeholders to try and ensure they had sufficient awareness of the Act. Simon was part of this process and I remember him at events in deep conversation with Baroness Ashton, the Minister who was responsible for the Act. And since 2007 Simon has continued to talk up the Act at events, conferences and in other public settings. In the course of doing this he has also made the links with other policies that relate to mental capacity such as direct payments and personal budgets, nor has he been shy of speaking out when the activities of government or other organisations look like they are having a detrimental impact on the lives of people with disabilities.

The Mental Health Foundation undertook a research project *Making Best Interests Decisions: People and Processes* with Bristol University that investigated how direct payments were being used by people who lacked capacity to request them and their families. Simon spoke at the launch of the research findings and an online resource for practitioners: *Indirect Payments for People Who Lack Capacity - How they Work in Practice*. He certainly didn't mince his words and spoke with great passion. I suspect he said things that others in the room were pleased to hear even though they wouldn't have been able to say it themselves, because of the organisations they were representing.

I know at times it's been difficult for Simon, not least because of health difficulties he has struggled with. Yet not only has he been remarkably stoical but he has also continued to offer his services despite these difficulties. Long may that continue.

So there you have it, Toby Williamson has also become a friend and very close work colleague. In the next section Dr. Lucy Series from Cardiff Law School outlines how I fought for some of the changes to the *Mental Capacity Act 2005*.

Dr Lucy Series, Research Associate at Cardiff Law School and Blogger writes:

The other evidence from a person with firsthand experience of the MCA comes from Simon Cramp, and is on p478 of the first volume of evidence. Simon describes himself as '42 years old and I have a learning disability and dyslexic and dyspraxia'. Simon is also a fellow of the Centre for Welfare Reform; I once had the pleasure of meeting Simon at a Housing and Support Alliance conference, he is a very active campaigner for rights to inclusion and self-determination. Simon submitted evidence to the Joint Committee on the draft *Mental Incapacity Bill*. He was involved in campaigning for some important changes to the original Bill, including getting the name changed from the *Mental Incapacity Bill* to the *Mental Capacity Act*; he also helped to campaign for the inclusion of advocacy (hence the IMCA service). Simon thinks that the impact of the MCA has been limited: 'after the great fanfare apart from court cases you hear very little in the media or online'.

Simon is critical of the quality of available online information about the MCA, and the depth of detail in the code of practice (he asks whether anyone except professionals ever read it). He suggests that the government should issue pocket book or cards, summarising the Act's core principles and people's responsibilities. Simon thinks there needs to be a publicity campaign on the Act, and that it might need updating to deal with developments in adult social care. He is critical of professionals' understanding of the MCA and he doesn't think it has fostered appropriate involvement of carers and families in decision making. This is what Simon has to say about the accessibility of the Office of the Public Guardian and the Court of Protection:

'...it is a joke that everything has to be filled in online as in my book if you have a disability and struggle to write this in a way that is easier for you. Then the issues about it more accessible online is laughable, it is about government saving money which is not what the principles of this Act is about, this Act is about giving people choice.'

So, more food for thought from Simon and the on the need to make the information and the administrative and legal apparatus of the MCA more accessible."

Here is an extract of the evidence I gave in parliament on the draft bill and the evidence I submitted before appearing in Parliament in 2003

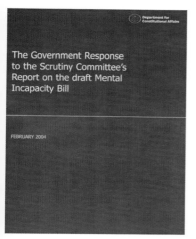

The Government Response to the Scrutiny Committee's Report on the draft Mental Incapacity Bill

FEBRUARY 2004

Scrutiny Committee report

Examination of Witnesses (Questions 680-699)

DR MAURICE BROOK, MRS MARY PEARSON, MR DAVID SUGDEN, MR JAMES ALLEN AND MR SIMON CRAMP

21 OCTOBER 2003

Q680 Baroness McIntosh of Hudnall: It has been put to us by other witnesses that this Bill as currently drafted is potentially more of a charter for carers and service providers than it is a protection for people who may lack capacity to make decisions. Do you have a view about that? Can you tell us from your experience how it would be best for people with incapacity to be informed about what the Draft Bill could do for them?

Mr Cramp: In the Bill, if it was possible, I would want to make it separate, where paid carers are separated from family carers. The state saves quite a lot because of parents who are unpaid carers but in terms of the question of abuse, if you work for an organisation and you abuse anything, you will be subject to some form of discipline. With a carer it is more difficult. There is no formal power and we strongly recommend that there is some kind of distinction between them.

Q685 Mrs. Browning: Simon Cramp was asking for us to try and define on the face of the Bill between the paid carer and the voluntary carer, usually a close family relative. In what context do you want us to make this distinction?

Mr. Cramp: If my parents were looking after me, I would want to make them unpaid carers. In a previous life, I used to work for social services, so that is where I see the paid carers. In terms of advocacy, there is a line where you get advocacy for the person. There are procedures, whatever the organisation or whatever is in parliamentary law, which are set in and they restrict what you can do. There is more of a legal footing if you abuse somebody in any criminal way. It is easy to go through the court system where family carers would find that perhaps more difficult.

41. Supplementary memorandum from Mr. Simon Cramp (MIB 1214)

Thank you for giving me the opportunity to speak at the oral evidence session of the Joint Committee on Tuesday, 21 October. I hope the Committee found my evidence useful. You asked me to provide written answers to appropriate questions which we did not have the opportunity to talk about in the session and to say more, where I could, on anything the Committee asked me about. I would like to comment further on the General Authority to Act, the Court of Protection, the need for independent advocacy and how to make the final Bill more accessible.

1. THE GENERAL AUTHORITY TO ACT

The General Authority as it is currently set out would allow almost anyone to do almost anything. I think the scope of this power and the types of decisions which should be made under it needs to be tightened.

People with a learning disability are very fearful of the wording "reasonably believes" and it should be changed. It needs to be clear in the Bill that if someone wants to make decisions on someone else's behalf, they would have to go through a number of tests to ensure that the person could not make the decision themselves.

> A distinction should also be drawn between paid and unpaid carers. It would be a safer power if paid staff had to work to a person-centred plan and keep records so that they were accountable for the decisions they made. I recognise this is not practical for family members to do on a day-to-day basis but they should have to ask for formal powers if they wanted to take big decisions such where a person should live when they leave home.

> I do not think we should rule out the whole Bill on the basis that the

General Authority part needs changing. The system we have at the moment is not acceptable to people with a learning disability and should be changed.

2. INDEPENDENT ADVOCATES

I don't think the draft Bill makes sufficient provision for the resolution of conflicts between carers and people who have difficulty making or communicating a decision.

It needs to be made clearer in the final Bill that people should be allowed to make their own decisions. Putting the principles at the start of the Bill would help.

But people who have difficulties making decisions also need to be able to access support from independent advocates when making big decisions. An independent advocate should be there to ensure the voice of the person with a learning disability is heard rather than as an alternative decision-maker. Wherever possible, this advocate should be of the person's choosing. Independent advocacy services should follow a national code of practice.

I would ask the Committee to please mention the need for advocacy in their report as people with a learning disability really do need it on the face of the Bill as a safeguard against having decisions made for them by someone else.

3. COURT OF PROTECTION

The Court of Protection needs to be accessible for people with a learning disability to challenge decisions made on their behalf. One way of making it more accessible would be to have a panel sitting at a regional level—perhaps made up of a mix of professions such as a lawyer, a parent and a social worker—which conducts its proceedings in a way that a person with a learning disability can understand so that going to Court is not so scary. The people from the Court will need to be trained properly on how to deal with people with a learning disability.

4. INFORMING PEOPLE WITH A LEARNING DISABILITY ABOUT THE BILL

People with a learning disability have not been well informed about the draft Bill and that is one of the reasons why they are so angry about it. It was really good to have an accessible version of the draft Bill but it wasn't as accessible as it should have been and didn't tell the whole story. We will need a proper accessible version of the final Bill and accessible documents, like the code of practice, when implementing the Bill. I think the Government should ask people with a learning disability to help write these. A steering group could be set up to advise the Government. The Government will also need to work with organisations like Mencap and others to consult and inform their members.

I'm proud of my contribution, making government sit up and take notice of people with a learning disability. Sometimes seemingly small changes are important.

Mental Capacity Act 2005

One of the things I, and others campaigned for was the change in name from the *Mental Incapacity Bill*, to the *Mental Capacity Act*. Dropping two letters makes a huge difference to how people think about and act in supporting the right people have to make decisions.

Perhaps one of the biggest contributions I have made is making sure that people in a position of influence always remember to listen to the voices of those with real experience of services and support, this is picked up by Andrew Cozens.

Andrew Cozens CBE, President ADSS 2003-4, Strategic Adviser LGA 2006-12 writes:

Simon has always been a disruptive influence in my professional life, and that is certainly not a bad thing. Meeting him is like facing up to that angel on your shoulder telling you that you have just ducked an issue or out something in the too hard to deal with or I might come back to it drawer. He is also brilliant at spotting waffle or policy-speak – "sorry Andrew but what does that really mean?" The chances are I do not know either!

I think I first met Simon when I was taking up national roles for the (then) Association of Directors of Social Services. Over the almost 20 years since we have picked up conversations in various places, shared platforms at conferences and workshops, and exchanged emails and articles on subjects close to his heart.

Looking back on our contact I can see the stop/start progress of policy and practice for people with learning disabilities and their carers as will be evident from other chapters and contributors. This period is bookended by *Valuing People* at one end and Winterbourne View at the other extreme. In between is populated by stories of individual achievements and system failures.

One such moment was the juxtaposition for me of the success of the 2012 Paralympics and the publication of the *Serious Case Review on Winterbourne View.*

The Serious Case Review was commissioned by South Gloucestershire where the private hospital was located and it summarised the individual reviews by the range of organisations with responsibility for case management or oversight, and made many challenging recommendations.

The Government also published interim conclusions and a final report followed in 2013.

I had two strong feelings reading these reports. The first was the depressing familiarity of the recommendations about the dangers of institutions and isolation from home, family and community. The second was that bigger policy issues could yet remain unaddressed.

It is disturbing to discover just how many similar places exist and how much is spent commissioning services from them. As a director I was aware of a small number of people in my area that my health service colleagues felt needed very specialist oversight by consultant psychiatry and nursing. We had sought to meet their needs when the previous long stay hospitals were replaced by community based services.

Different areas took different approaches with some services remaining in the NHS and others developed with voluntary and independent organisations. What I had not grasped was the extent to which this provision had steadily become a national service, with people often being placed a long way from their roots.

Repeated studies have shown the risks that distance and a lack of case management or advocacy can bring. This was exacerbated by a similar detachment of the board responsible for these services. In many respects patients and staff seemed out of sight and out of mind.

The Paralympics' ambition was to transform our society's view of disability. Winterbourne View reminded us of that we must pay the closest attention to the interests of those furthest from home, family and independence and bring fresh impetus to new models of care and support for them.

I remember reflecting with Simon on how this had happened and his take was typically direct. No one talked directly to those needing such services, their voices were not heard and commissioners just did not know what was being done in their name.

Most recently I caught up with Simon in Bournemouth. He apologised that he had to dash off to meet Jon Rouse, Director General in the Department for Health. That was one of a number of people he had secured time with. I know they will have had something to reflect on after the meeting. I always did and tried to act on it, even though it was invariably uncomfortable to face up to.

More power to his elbow!

Chapter 7 Housing

Simon on a Housing and Support Alliance stall

I know that the world of Westminster can seem a long way from real life for a lot of people so as well as campaigning for changes in the law, I've always been keen to be involved in the things which really help people with learning disabilities; having the right support and living somewhere you choose are important for anyone. I was extremely proud to receive a lifetime membership of the newly formed Learning Disability England for my contribution to the Housing and Support Alliance. I've been involved in housing and support in a lot of ways; here are some reflections from colleagues I've worked with.

David Abbey, Managing Director MySafeHome writes

I first met Simon at a conference over 10 years ago and it's been a real pleasure getting to know him, especially during the 12 months he worked for us here at MySafeHome as a part-time Field Marketing Adviser.

Sadly we had to make him redundant when lenders stopped providing mortgages for the HOLD (Home Ownership for people with

Long-term Disabilities) model – a unique Government approved and funded housing option that gives people with disabilities the chance to buy a home of their own – that we're here to support. Whilst the redundancy process was obviously an unsettling and uncertain period Simon continued to fulfil his responsibilities in a typically professional and calm manner.

As one of MySafeHome's public faces Simon played a vital role in continuing to enhance our reputation as well as promoting the many benefits of home ownership for people with disabilities, everything from freedom of choice through to greater independence and security of tenure. Tasked with identifying and engaging with key stakeholders across the disability and housing sectors as well as explaining the positive benefits (for appropriate people) that home ownership brings for all concerned Simon well and truly tackled the role with gusto.

Contributing to the development of our marketing activities he was a natural at identifying any opportunities and knew precisely how to make the most of one of his key strengths, verbal reasoning. With this skill under his belt he was never afraid to ask the kind of questions that others might not, he was also a born networker who was clearly both well-known and well-liked throughout the Learning Disability sector (a reputation he still enjoys to this day). Bringing together all of these facets of his personality he contributed to a range of activities that directly led to dozens of people with disabilities having the chance to choose how and where they live their lives, something that only home ownership really delivers.

Simon instinctively understood how owning a home of your own could really change your life, especially where individuals were either living in the family home with elderly parents who were no longer able to provide the care and support that they needed or in residential facilities, sometimes hundreds of miles away from where they grew up. In the worst case scenarios they were effectively 'locked up' in Assessment and Treatment Units such as the now vilified Winterbourne View, scene of some truly horrific acts of abuse, and the work that Simon did helped ensure that when the time came we were able to help several residents of this and similar Units to move on to homes of their own. On top of all of the benefits that HOLD delivers to buyers Simon also appreciated that the model could work out to be far more cost effective too, in some cases leading to savings of over £100,000 per person per year. All this and a future that buyers could really look forward to, Simon seized on these deliverables and well and truly made it his mission to help spread the word.

Since leaving us in 2011 we've remained firm friends and Simon generously continues to share what's happening within the disability sector generally and how this might impact on home ownership. We don't always get to meet as often as we should but continue to see each other at conferences and other events during the year, which is always a real pleasure.

Seeing the huge difference that home ownership makes to people with disabilities Simon's always gone out of his way to assist us however he can, both as an employee and in his own free time. With mortgage lending still currently a real challenge it's good to know that he's always on the lookout for fresh opportunities or mulling over new ideas for how to tackle the problem. This willingness to support others and make a real difference wherever he can is typical of Simon and you can't help feeling that whatever he goes on to do next his legacy will be felt for many, many years to come.

Alicia Wood, former CEO of Housing and Support Alliance writes:

'Who is this cocky northern bloke?' I thought when I first met Simon Cramp. We were at a Housing Options Away Day for members in 2002 (I think) in Birmingham. Simon was co-chairing the event with David Wolverson from Dimensions who was at the time, the Chair of Housing Options. At that time, Housing Options operated as a charity that helped people with learning disabilities and families alongside around 50 members that were mainly housing and care providers with a few local authorities. We were totally apolitical and we did not involve people with learning disabilities or families (though some staff were parents and siblings of people with learning disabilities) in the running of our organisation or events that we held, except as the occasional passive participant.

So the be-suited and dapper Simon Cramp sat at the front of a room full of about 50 members and made very clear that as a man with a learning disability, he had something important to say and that he was not going to mince his words. He declared his political allegiance and gave an uncomfortable account of the lack of regard politics has had for people with learning disabilities, the housing, social care and benefits system that often works against people with learning disabilities having a good life. He told us professionals to sort ourselves out, otherwise people with learning disabilities would continue to be treated as second class citizens.

There was a lot of squirming and discomfort in that room. At that time (pre social media), we were unused to hearing uncensored truths about the professional world we inhabit and our part in it. People with learning disabilities and families that spoke at events were expected to tell their story, talk about the good things we professionals did for them and be polite. Professionals were expected to keep political opinions to themselves and never criticise or challenge too strongly. Simon did none of this and I became a big fan of his from that moment.

With my great friend Alicia Wood

Simon has since been a volunteer and friend of Housing Options and later when we became the Housing & Support Alliance in 2012 he volunteered for us. Simon keeps us updated on news relating to people with learning disabilities and politics, his area of expertise and interest. He has also spoken and volunteered at our conferences and events. Simon has used his own experience to advocate for others with learning disabilities but has also uniquely been able to advocate for people with more complex learning disabilities because of his experience with his twin brother, who sadly died last year.

Probably what I value most about Simon is that he is an independent thinker. So many assumptions are made about what people with learning disabilities can and can't do and Simon defies all of the stereotypes. He has a great mind and can put together and communicate arguments well but despite being so capable, he tells us how much help he needs to get by on a day to day basis and function independently. But he is unlikely to ever get the help he needs except from his family because the social care system simply doesn't work for more able people with learning disabilities. This is something that Simon often speaks about and challenges us all on.

Simon is also a world class networker. He knows everyone and everyone knows him. He is a canny manoeuvrer, putting people in touch with each other, getting people and organisations to do things and constantly working for the good of people with learning disabilities despite being independent and not part of a formal group. He usually does not get paid for his efforts and this is something that often troubles me about Simon. How can someone with so much talent, knowledge and skills be unemployed when we have so many people working in our field that don't even have a tenth of what Simon has? Maybe this is caught up with the problem that so many people with mild learning disabilities have - being too able to get the help they need.

Simon reminds me a bit of my Dad, a cocky northern bloke too, in that self-confidence that enables people to just say what they think and believe in their own views. He recently saved me when there was a technical problem in our annual conference while I was supposed to be showing a film and he took the mic and spoke to the audience for 10 minutes as if he had pulled a well rehearsed speech out of his pocket. I wish I could be a bit more like that.

Oh and I almost forgot, he gives a bloomin' good hug and asks 'how are you love?' as he gives it and you just know he means it.

Chapter 8 **Freedom**

I am a Fellow of the Centre for Welfare Reform, a place where many of my collaborations and publications are found; here Simon Duffy explains some of our work together.

Simon Duffy, Director of the Centre for Welfare Reform writes:

I only got to know Simon after I moved down to Sheffield, after working in Scotland for many years. At that time I was leading a national project called In Control and I was trying to persuade both local and national government that we should change the social care system so that everybody got a personal budget, which they could control as they wished. We called this new system self-directed support.

I think it was at a conference where I was speaking about self-directed support when I first met Simon. He had been talking to people about the changes in the law that he had been involved in helping make happen - which would eventually be called the *Mental Capacity Act*. This was very important because it should help people remember that everybody, absolutely everybody, has the right to make their own decisions or to have the most appropriate person represent them if they need representation. Quite rightly Simon tackled me at the conference to ask me about whether I knew about the changes to the new *Mental Capacity Act*. I had to admit I had not been paying much attention to it and so Simon suggested we meet to think about how the *Mental Capacity Act* affected self-directed support. This seemed like a really good idea.

At the time Simon was working for Dimensions and he used to come into Sheffield quite often and, as I live in Sheffield, we agreed to meet in the Dimensions office in Sheffield in order to talk things over. Once we got talking it was clear that the *Mental Capacity Act* and self-directed support did fit together quite well. They were both about giving more power to people with learning disabilities. However it also looked like there was going to be two big problems.

69

Problem Number 1 was that lots of people did need help to manage a personal budget.

Problem Number 2 was that lots of people might need representation, but they didn't need this to be done by setting up an official representative through the courts. This would be too expensive, slow and unnecessarily bureaucratic. So we wanted to help people see other solutions that would help people keep decisions close to the person.

The solution we came up with was what is sometimes called 'supported decision-making' - which means making sure people have all the help they need to make their own decisions, however complex their disability. However we rewrote this recently and called it, more simply, the 7 Principles of Freedom:

1. Capacity - you must start by assuming I have the ability to be in control
2. Specific - even if I cannot make some decisions I may still be able to make others
3. Selection - if I need a representative I should be able to pick them
4. Suitable - any representative should be right for me and my needs
5. Best Interest - any representative must look after my best interests
6. Involvement - I always have the right to be involved in any decisions
7. Review - all arrangements must be reviewed and improved over time

We often forget that we all need help and assistance to be in control. Some people just need extra support. So, if you are supporting someone then please remember these principles.

It was great working with Simon on this project and very quickly the paper we wrote became one of the most important papers from my time at In Control. It really helped social workers and families to have a fresh think about decisions and capacity. Simon and I kept talking about this paper and Simon encouraged me to rewrite our earlier work as *Freedom: a guide to good support*. Simon kindly wrote the Foreword to that guide.

Over the next few years Simon and I stayed in touch and Simon was an important national advocate for In Control. He saw how important this project was at setting a new standard for how society should support people with learning difficulties. Simon was also very helpful in spotting what was going on nationally and in Parliament. Simon and I have continued to meet regularly and talk about the state of the world. I was pleased to support Simon and Don Derrett as they began Self-Direct. Together they, and their other colleagues, did great work at showing what was possible with self-directed support. As ever with Simon, the focus was on offering people practical next steps and respecting the positive role that service providers could play.

I think that is one of the things that I like about working with Simon. On the one hand Simon has strong moral convictions and is clearly interested in the rights of people with learning difficulties. On the other hand Simon is not someone who just bad mouths people because of their role or job title. He doesn't write off all families just because some families struggle. He doesn't write-off all service providers just because some do a bad job. Simon is more interested in what people really do than what they say.

Simon was also a great ally when I left In Control in 2009. I had run the project for 6 years but I found that many people thought I was too critical of Government and they felt that I should take a back seat. So when I resigned it was really nice that people like Simon, Don and many others stood by me.

A few months later I set up the Centre for Welfare Reform and this is what I am still doing today. I wanted to find a new way of sharing good ideas and linking good people. Very early on I asked Simon whether he would like to become a Fellow of the Centre and I was very pleased that he agreed. Over the past 6 years Simon has not only been supportive, he has also helpfully shared some of his own experiences and this has led to important information being shared on the Centre's website. In particular, with Self Direct we helped with the publication of two very important books: *Self-direction: The Key to a Better Life* and *Helping Providers to Change*.

Unfortunately the new Government in 2010 started to cut funding for social care and for new initiatives like self-directed support. It became harder and harder to earn a living for organisations like Self Direct.

In fact, over the past few years, it has been hard to get away from the dreadful political situation faced by people with learning difficulties. This was why, in 2014, Simon and I worked together to create the

Learning Disability Alliance (now Learning Disability England). This is an exciting movement to bring together people with learning difficulties, families professionals and other allies.

Simon gave some fantastic speeches at the events we ran - really challenging people to wake up to what was going on and step up to the need for leadership. It is still early days for Learning Disability England but Simon's support was very important.

Overall Simon has always been able to balance challenge with support. Simon knows he can tell me - quite bluntly - if he thinks I'm doing things wrong. He's not afraid to tell me my writing is too complex or question my strategies. But he's also able to see the bigger picture and to tell those who really want to make things better from those who just like the sound of their own voice. I look forward to many more years, fighting the good fight, together.

Here's my preface to *Freedom: a guide to good support*:

Front cover of *Freedom*

Most people take freedom as a given. But for someone with a learning disability that is not always the case. This means that there often more controls and fewer choices. People miss out on some of the most important things in life.

A lot has happened in my life. I have a learning disability; but I am passionate about politics and the rights of people with learning disabilities. I bought my first newspaper when I was fourteen years old - The Guardian. Often I went without my lunch to afford it and would rush out of school to go and buy it.

I have kept trying to contribute and to give something back to the community and to stick up for people like me and others who have even more severe disabilities. For many years people with learning disabilities and their allies have been campaigning for the right for people to have more control over their own lives. In response to this, in England the government published a consultation document, *Supported Decisions* and then a further paper, *Who Decides?*

In 2003 Parliament set up a Joint Committee in order to review the draft legislation on mental capacity (which at the time was called the Mental Incapacity Bill). I wrote to the committee, with the support of Mencap, and then was invited to speak to the committee at the Palace of Westminster. It was a nerve-wracking experience; but I was able to argue that people should have a clear 'right to advocacy' and there should be better safeguards for people with severe disabilities. There were then some important changes made to the final legislation.

I was very proud that I was one of the first people with learning disabilities ever to speak to a committee in Westminster.

Then in 2005 I worked with Simon Duffy, the author of this report, to publish an important paper on self-determination and individual budgets . We explained how it was possible for people with learning disabilities to control their lives, including any budget for their support.

I have been lucky. I was given the chance to exercise control and be in control of my own life. There have been many had low points, and many plus points, but I was very lucky to have had good parents and the support of friends and family. But some people are not so lucky.

I hope and pray that one day everyone - whether or not you have a learning disability - will have freedom. Choice and control should be a given. We should not have to keep fighting for our freedom

Chapter 9 **What Next?**

For much of my life I have been campaigning to make the lives of people with learning difficulties better. My campaigns have been targeted at organisations, both government and private, in the hope that those organisations do not make decisions *for* people with learning disabilities, but actually listen to what is said so that decisions are made *with* people.

I know that my campaigns have made a small difference, but I don't think that I will ever see the time when organisations will listen fully, and they will also continue to make decisions based on assumptions of what is best for others.

I know that there are many things in my everyday life that I struggle with. Simple things that most people can manage without thinking, things that require a level of manual dexterity, understanding systems, reading and writing and planning to get from A to B are usually things that require a great deal of effort and support. I am aware that when explaining my thoughts, or issues with others I can be long winded, this is because I have a need for others to understand my thought process. If I am interrupted, when in full flow, I can lose my thread and have to start from the beginning again. This is the way my mind works.

I know that I can become fixated on my health, and do tend to be negative. I have been a clumsy person all my life, and it was only in the last 10 years that a name has been given to my difficulties, dyspraxia, and although just having the name doesn't make life easier, it does help me to understand myself a little better.

Luckily I have a level of family support that helps me to partially manage some of the difficulties that I have. These are the things that I have to live with and manage the best way I can. I may be awkward, clumsy, make mistakes. I can put my thoughts into writing, but these often make no sense to anyone until they are edited and clarified.

Despite my difficulties, I know that I am able to consider properly the issues that affect me, and other people with a learning disability or difficulty, and to work with others to find sensible solutions to any problems that there may be. I am an individual, but can work with others. I need some time to research issues, and need a level of support to talk over my thoughts, before reaching something like a solution. I may have a learning difficulty but I am not stupid.

I will continue to do what I do, for as long as I can, and for as long as people listen. I feel that I can do more, given the right opportunities. All important steps forward in life can only be made acceptable and valuable if the steps are reached following real consultation and evaluation. Thankfully society have moved away from the principle of 'doing good' to those parts of society that need a level of help. I would like to be involved in the planning and provision of services for people that are of real value to them. How that takes place I cannot answer, but I am sure that all valuable and beneficial solutions to problems take place when the providers, the funders and the recipients all get together and find the right solution for everyone.

I am a person with a learning disability. I am not stupid. I am not someone who wishes to be a burden on society, as I can contribute something. I am not someone who is there to be made a profit out of. Working together, working for each other, working to make the best of what skills we have and working together to make our society the best we can.

We still have a fight on our hands, people with disabilities are still left out, treated badly and targeted by this Conservative Government to face the burden of the cuts. We can't stop fighting. We need to work together now more than ever. What next? Lord Cramp of Chesterfield would be nice...

Chapter 10 **Collected Writings**

Christmas Reflections

I used to live with my parents. But then one day my Mum said "you have to move into your own place." She said: "I am not going to be around forever."

It really freaked me out! I went upstairs and cried. I was just so scared about the future and the thought of losing her. I moved in with my twin brother. I've been helping to look after him since he had a heart attack.

Then 2 years ago Mum died. She was 63. And then my Gran died 3 months later! So it was a horrible time. My Mum had quite a few health problems. But it was still a shock when she died. When I told my boss at work he offered to clear his diary and come and support me at the funeral. Things like that mean a lot. You need friends around you as a circle of support. Christmas is a very sad time for me, before it was always a happy time. But now it just reminds me of people who have died.

You have to find the inner strength to cope. I've come though it all. I'm still hanging on in there. You just have to get on with it and do the best you can.

Just About Managing?

A blog about the Autumn Statement 2016. Well I was a busy bee. I went to three conferences in the space of a week.

The money thing I went to the people do what they call how the money might be spent, the booklet was over 200 pages long lots of complicated stuff to understand and I went to a briefing to explain to me what it meant by the people who wrote the report and what they call the Autumn Statement. Both reports were very complicated - but as some of the newspapers said and people who are commentators - it was strange and fool hardy for them not to give any money for social care or NHS and I think the Government is putting off the difficult decisions a bit like they did not decided till recently what to do of how to fund elderly care, and with the problem of the care act 2014 stated that you are entitled to a community care assessment and that there is then no money for council to spend on what care you need! If your needs are not critical or substantial in your disability then the system as, Simon Duffy says, is already broken. I think it snapped in two and need some very strong Gaffa Tape or super glue or to start again and put money in and for the Government to not blame everyone else. I lay the blame at the Government door as welfare policy seems designed to hit those who couldn't fight back.

Finally the beginning of the following week I went to Learning Disability Today Conference it was my 14th year, mainly speaking and chairing, it takes a lot of planning and preparation if you are running a session, it was full on. Read my special blog where I describe the way you have to get ready for this big event. But when I got home I could sleep for a week.

The Winning Formula

This is a special blog about what it is like to be part of the programme of organising a session or speaking at Learning Disability Today London and what is involved.

Well where do I start! I have done both over a 14 year association with the event. It is not a case of just turning up on the day there is lots of planning that goes into it. First as speaker you are given a brief of what they want you to focus on what you want to say. With others in a particular session this often at least 3 speakers and chair and that could be a mixture of people with learning disability a professional CEO or an academic, or all three. This is at least a month to six week before the event and you have to ask who is saying what. I like to see what others are saying then often someone has decided to change what they were say at last min! Also you might be asked to step in at very short notice like less than 12 hours which happened at this year's event. This year I did three sessions of one hour as well as catching up with friends old and new. It is quite stressful, but less so if you have the winning formula, which is three simple things. If you stick to them you will go far:

1. A real good event organiser /and chair of your session
2. You have planned everything that could work and not work and you are prepared
3. Finally that you make sure your material is understandable to everyone, people with a learning disability and professionals.

My Week in the Big Smoke

London: 14th March to the 18th March 2016. Well what a week that has been in the work of learning disability. On Monday a relaxing day travelling down to London and settling in to a great hotel near the train station at London St. Pancras for a great price. A good night's sleep and a great breakfast to start my first day of work on the Tuesday at a conference on safeguarding in residential settings - discussing the issues with people and key agencies from health and social services. There were stands from Mencap on wills and trusts and an exciting organisation who is thinking outside the box, Talking Mats.

The Budget was the centre piece of the week and how the Chancellor, the money man, delivered his programme and goals including ideas of cutting benefits while offering money to be paid to people who have pots of money. By Monday of the following week, Iain Duncan Smith had walked out of the Department for Work and Pensions, on welfare policy. The Money Man, the Chancellor, is having to come up with a plan B by Tuesday on cuts to benefits.

It all centred on the Government idea of wanting to reduce or cut Personal Independence Payment and yet give a tax cut to those who could afford to pay more - as you can imagine twitter and facebook went into mayhem - there was anger not just from disabled people themselves, but from financial experts and MPs saying it is simply a step too far.

So yesterday Tuesday on the 22nd March 2016 in the House of Commons to sign off the main changes and then get what they called the Finance Bill through parliament once MPs say yes to it. And last night the Government had to admit it had egg on its face after so many people got really upset and angry. And the leading group of money experts said that the Government plans on benefits, should the Government have pushed it through, wouldn't actually save any money. But this developing story on welfare will develop over the coming months; my sense is that the Government will not move forward with the proposal on Personal Independence Payment. Let's not kid ourselves that although they say it is off the table for the rest of parliament, there will be another fight I suspect on welfare in the future. When will the Government learn about saying one thing to win a headline, 'We are all in this together' but then to keep hitting people with learning disability? So I guess watch this space.

On the Friday of the week we had a conference on transforming lives for people with learning disability and it was leads in the field, and one change to the programme Rob Greig was asked to do a session on employment and he suggested that perhaps people with learning disability could work but we the sector don't help the people who could work.

It was an interesting week with lots of themes and more to digest over the next coming months and years until 2020.

We don't learn from past mistakes.

In this guest blog, Simon Cramp says the latest Care Quality Commission report on Southern Health shows how lessons from past mistakes have not been learnt – and that this has to stop.

Another week, another report on failings at Southern Health NHS Foundation Trust and the debacle of Justice for LB.

The background to this case is well known. Connor Sparrowhawk – 'Laughing Boy' or 'LB' for short – drowned in a bath while at an assessment and treatment unit run by Southern Health in 2013. There followed an inquest, serious case review and then an independent report in December 2015 by Mazars, which was commissioned by NHS England. The Mazars report pulled no punches on the failings at the trust.

Now, we have had a report by the Care Quality Commission (CQC) of its latest inspection of Southern Health, conducted over 4 days in January.

The critical report highlighted serious concerns about the safety of patients with mental health problems and learning disabilities in some locations operated by Southern Health. The CQC's inspection found that many of the previously reported failings – especially in relation to governance, patient safety and ability to respond to patient concerns – were still evident.

In addition, the board of Southern Health were criticised for showing little evidence of being proactive in identifying risk to the people it cares for or of taking action to address that risk before concerns are raised by external bodies.

The report is very powerful and the question is how does it move on the issues of stopping things like reducing sudden deaths and making sure when they do happen the process is more transparent and that due process is done correctly – i.e. deaths are properly investigated?

It was interesting that on the eve of the report being published the chair of the board of Southern Health, Mike Petter, resigned.

Meanwhile, Sara Ryan, Connor's mother, has done her own audit, based on a template from the National Audit Office:

I would be very unhappy as a worker and as a service user to get this sort of service.

At Southern Health the troops on the ground are working really hard – as the

CQC report noted –while the leadership is seemingly non-existent. I would call on Southern Health's CEO, Katrina Percy, to ask herself the question that Andrea Sutcliffe, chief inspector of adult care at the CQC, always poses: would I be happy for my mum or dad to use these services?

I bet this service doesn't meet the Mum Test. There is a big rebuilding job to do at the trust and Health Secretary Jeremy Hunt and the board of Southern Health have questions to answer. They keep referring to something that was being promised and implemented last December and yet there are still problems.

As a service user, I would not put up with this and we don't seem to learn from past mistakes and scandals because they keep on happening. It has got to stop.

Publications

Simon's writing and contributions are too numerous to list in their entirety. Many are collated on his profile page on the Centre for Welfare Reform's website:

www.centreforwelfarereform.org/about-us/centre-fellows/simon-cramp.html

Also a quick Google search of 'Simon Cramp UK' gives some indication of his many contributions to: Parliamentary Scrutiny Committees, Conferences, Reviews and insightful blogs.

Acknowledgments

I will always be grateful to Brian Rix, later in life Lord Rix. The man was an inspiration to me and helped me become the person I am today. He was very encouraging, we both worked together on that fateful day in 1998 when we both helped the Mencap family change its rules to allow people with a learning disability to contribute to the governance of Mencap. Brian used his wit and charisma to lead from the front. He helped me do my small bit to make Mencap the organisation it is today. I will always remember you Brian, may you rest in peace.

I also dedicate this book to some people who are role models and people I look up to: Simon Duffy, Steve Scown, David Wolverson, Andrew Cozens, Richard Banks, David Abbey, Don Derrett, Alicia Wood, Jackie Lawley and everyone at Learning Disability England. Finally, my Dad, Howard Cramp.

Publishing Information

Don't Cramp My Style © Simon Cramp 2017.
Edited by Tim Keilty.
Adapted from a design by Henry Iles.
www.henryiles.com
Don't Cramp My Style is published by the Centre for Welfare Reform.
www.centreforwelfarereform.org
First published November 2017

Excerpts from Mencap publications are reproduced with permission from Royal Mencap Society.
84 pp
ISBN 978-1-907790-98-0

Printed by BoD'in Norderstedt, Germany